DRIVERS ON DRIVERS

Motorsport greats on their rivals, teammates and heroes

Porter Press International

© **Porter Press International**

All rights reserved. No part of this publication may be reproduced, stored in a retrieval system or transmitted, in any form or by any means, electronic, mechanical, photocopying, recording or otherwise, without prior permission in writing from the publisher.

First published November 2021

ISBN 978-1-913089-41-2

Published by Porter Press International Ltd

Hilltop Farm, Knighton-on-Teme,
Tenbury Wells, WR15 8LY, UK
Tel: +44 (0)1584 781588
sales@porterpress.co.uk
www.porterpress.co.uk

Edited by James Page
Design by Wayne Batty
Printed by Gomer Press Ltd

Copyright

We have made every effort to trace and acknowledge copyright holders and apologise in advance for any unintentional omission. We would be pleased to insert the appropriate acknowledgement in any subsequent edition.

Acknowledgements

First and foremost, I would like to thank very sincerely all those interviewed in this book. Without them, it would look a little bare!

I would also like to thank my distinguished colleagues who assisted with interviews for this book – namely, Peter Windsor, Ben Edwards, Louise Goodman, Mark Cole, Ian Wagstaff, Simon Taylor and, above all, David Tremayne, who conducted no fewer than five.

I am grateful to Abigail Humphries, Louise Gibbs, Annelise Airey, Mark Woolley, Serge Vanbockryck, Erika Wooding and Martin Brundle for various assistance.

My colleague Wayne Batty has, as you can see, done a superb job on designing this book.

I wish to acknowledge the generous support, with the supply of photographs, of Motorsport Images, Dr David Wright (Brian Kent Joscelyne Collection), Corporate Archives Porsche AG, Michael Cole, Ian Wagstaff and Steve Havelock.

James Page, in editing this book, has brought to bear not only his considerable skills in that department but also his vast knowledge of motor racing, plus wise counsel. Furthermore, he has contributed the profiles and captions.

My long-suffering wife, Julie, has put up with yet another book (!) and the impact such imposes.

Finally, my very sincere thanks to the great Ross Brawn, who has contributed a very generous and wonderfully supportive foreword.

Philip Porter, November 2021

FOREWORD

This is a very different book, which is absolutely fascinating. It is the brainchild of Philip Porter, whom I have known for a number of years. I am delighted it is supporting Hope for Tomorrow, of which I am a Patron.

Philip and his superb team of motor racing writers have gathered a positive *Who's Who?* of motorsport, spread over every decade from the 1950s to the present day. In these pages you will hear from more than a dozen World Champions and others who had highly distinguished careers in a variety of different fields.

I am proud to say I know, or have known, all of them and worked with many. Stirling was a good friend. I knew Graham Hill when he had his own team, and Jackie Oliver gave me my first job as a Technical Director. Alan Jones was one of the first drivers I worked with when I was a mechanic.

It is a fascinating book because you hear all these brilliant drivers describing their rivals, their friends and their teammates in their own words. There are candid opinions which are revealing and intriguing. Despite my many years in motor racing, they are almost all totally new insights for me, as I am sure they will be for you.

This is a book you can dip-in and dip-out of, or read from cover to cover. I suspect, though, you will find it difficult to put down.

I wholeheartedly recommend this book because it features some great names, is compelling reading and is supporting Hope for Tomorrow, which does a wonderful job providing mobile cancer units.

Ross Brawn OBE

CONTENTS

INTRODUCTION	7
Damon **HILL**	8
Mario **ANDRETTI**	14
Jackie **STEWART**	18
Tony **BROOKS**	24
George **RUSSELL**	28
Allan **McNISH**	30
David **COULTHARD**	36
Gerhard **BERGER**	38
Jackie **OLIVER**	44
Jamie **CHADWICK**	48
Alan **JONES**	50
Mark **BLUNDELL**	54
Brian **REDMAN**	56
Derek **WARWICK**	60
Lando **NORRIS**	68
Emerson **FITTIPALDI**	70
Derek **BELL**	74
Tim **PARNELL**	82
Mark **WEBBER**	84
Andy **WALLACE**	88
Emanuele **PIRRO**	90
Paddy **HOPKIRK**	96
Ray **BELLM**	100
David **HOBBS**	102
Mika **HÄKKINEN**	110
Richard **ATTWOOD**	114
Jody **SCHECKTER**	116
John **FITZPATRICK**	122
Lewis **HAMILTON**	128
Martin **BRUNDLE**	130
Stirling **MOSS**	136

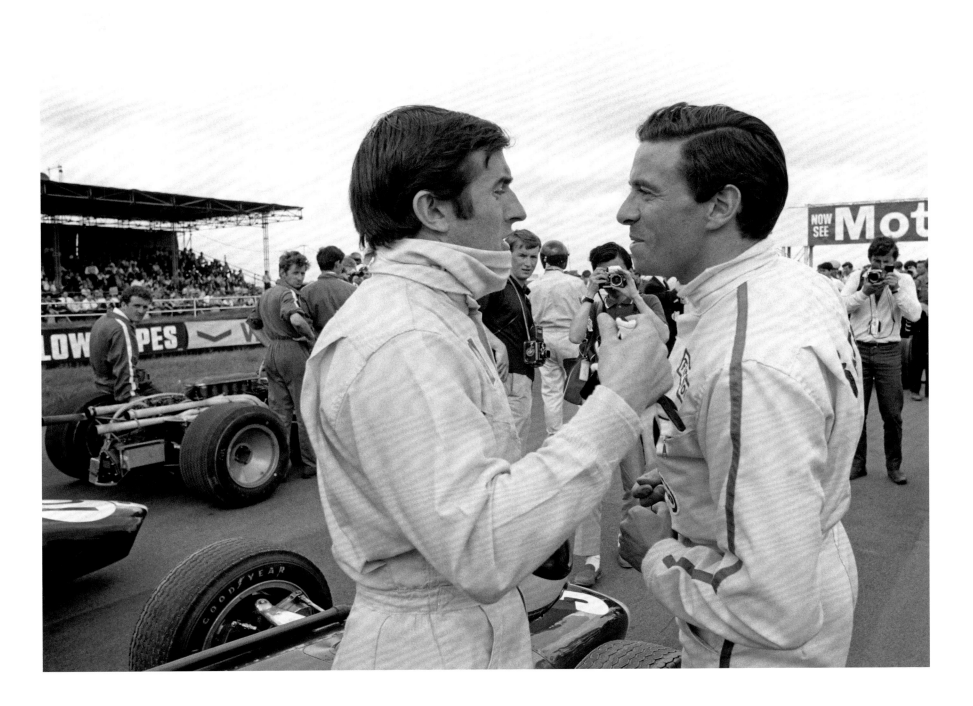

INTRODUCTION

I had the idea for this book about three years ago. The respected colleagues to whom I mentioned the notion reacted very positively, which encouraged me to take the plunge.

From the start, it was to be a book for charity. But which charity? I'd had a super relationship with Prostate Cancer UK for five years as their Motoring Ambassador, but felt this project needed a charity more aligned with motor racing. I first came across Hope for Tomorrow through my dear friend Stirling Moss, who was always very supportive – Chrissy Mills, the founder, being a great friend of Stirling and Susie's. With Patrons Ross Brawn, Martin Brundle, Derek Bell and David Richards, there was no doubting the motorsport connection. I have also worked on books with Ross, Martin and Derek.

So, off we went. Though I knew quite a few of the 'victims' in the book, there are a number I did not and had no intro to. This is where my distinguished journalist colleagues stepped in and added considerably to the cast list.

As to the content, my aim has been a happy balance of interesting, punchy and sometimes revealing comments. I was certainly not searching for, or expecting, anything scandalous. Equally, I hoped for something more than a bland, 'He was a nice guy'.

I believe every interview has its own character. I think it is interesting how different people have contrasting things to say about the same person. This just shows they were personal experiences. There is more to being a successful racing driver than car control, lightning reactions and balance. The mindset has to be right as well. As you will learn in these pages, there were drivers who had confidence, lacked confidence, played mind games, and suffered from mind games.

And then there was the humour! So necessary in any activity, it was particularly so during the period when motor racing was extremely dangerous.

There were also light-hearted moments during the creation of this book. Apart from laughing with many of the victims as they kindly told me, and my colleagues, amusing stories, the modern transcribing software I battled with to turn the spoken word into text threw up some, shall we say, 'eccentric' translations. If I may, I will share some examples with you...

our centre – Ayrton Senna
alhambra – Alain Prost
loveseat – Laffite
shoe market – Schumacher
oxygen mask – Jochen Mass
B&Q – Bianchi
among wealthy people – Emanuele Pirro
European grumpies – European Grands Prix
grab them – Brabham
chat room – Tertre Rouge
hamster – Hans Stuck
my experience – Mike Spence
prostitution – Prost and Senna
Phuket – Piquet
real nerve – Villeneuve
karate boxers – Colotti 'box
Stephanie Evans – Stefan Johansson
khaki rosebug – Keke Rosberg
we shaved the birds – we came third

You get my drift! You see, ladies and gentlemen, with what I had to contend to bring you this volume. I very much hope you will enjoy the book. If all goes well, I have a series in mind.

I will finish with what I believe to be a wonderful quote from Juan Manuel Fangio:

'Varzi was to me a god... he is probably the driver I have admired most in my life, a man who cared only for his art.'

DAMON HILL

Interviewed by **PHILIP PORTER**

DAMON HILL (GB)
Born 17 September 1960

Damon Hill started his motorsport career on two wheels before switching to cars. He progressed through Formula Ford to Formula Three, and finished third in the 1988 British F3 Championship. Having become a test driver for the Williams Grand Prix team in 1991, Hill was promoted to a race seat two years later alongside Alain Prost. In 1994, he led Williams through one of its most traumatic seasons following the death of new teammate Ayrton Senna, and his battles with Michael Schumacher defined mid-1990s Formula One. In 1996, Hill followed in the footsteps of his father, Graham, by winning the World Championship, and by the time he retired in 1999 he'd won 22 Grands Prix.

Do you think racing drivers have evolved over time?

'There's something fundamentally the same about racing drivers through the ages. But they definitely have changed, the world has changed around them, and they've changed to suit that world, haven't they? I mean, the young guys today, how would you compare them to the Hunts or the Mosses or the Fangios? A completely different set of concerns, it seems to me.'

Rather more politically correct?

'Lewis has become politically aware, but you wouldn't have got a driver in the 1960s or '50s doing something like that. They used to race anywhere and turn a blind eye. It wasn't seen that your responsibilities as a sports person were to the world around you. They just got on with their lives and raced all over the place. Fascist dictatorships didn't matter. There wasn't any choice anyway, if you wanted to be a global sportsman.'

Of course Fangio was abducted in Cuba.

'Yeah, by the revolutionaries. He was the epitome of diplomacy, wasn't he? I mean, he never managed to cause controversy at all about anything. He was brilliant at that. So some of them now, reluctantly, are drawn into it. But social media has just completely changed their world as well. They have the ability to speak out on anything they want to. They are beyond the command of, as Dylan would say, sons and daughters, they are beyond the command of the team's control, in some ways, with their social media, but then they realise that they've got this responsibility. So in many ways, they're more sophisticated than, I would say, the '70s crew and the '80s crew. And the culture is less hedonistic. It was [previously] pretty much celebrated: the more frivolous you were with your life, the better it seemed.'

We look back and think they were fantastic characters, which they were, like your father and Innes Ireland – wonderful, larger-than-life, wild characters. It made them seem much more interesting than some rather bland guy saying all the correct PR things he should be saying.

'Today they allude to the fun they have but they are very careful about not getting caught because anywhere they go, or anything they do, is now on social media. We saw what happened with Nikita Mazepin: he tweeted, rather recklessly, a stupid, thoughtless tweet and one that probably embarrassed the poor girl quite a lot. And now he's having to get on his hands and knees and beg for forgiveness. Well, if that was James Hunt, back in the '70s, it would have been seen in a different way. I'm not saying it was right, but my dad, I'm afraid, would probably have been in deep trouble every other week.

'What they regarded as just being saucy and was all fun and games, now we see it maybe for what it really was. I don't know. And so there's other worries for drivers. They're much more restricted and conscious of their messaging than they ever were.'

And also commentators. I've always thought your father would have made the most fantastic pundit. When one thinks back to James Hunt, one of my favourite lines was when he said, 'Well, that's just the sort of pig ignorance you'd expect from Jarier!' Imagine anyone saying that today.

'Yeah [laughing]. It's the kind of thing we're used to now with Twitter, and trolls, aren't we? I wouldn't be allowed to say something like that on Sky.

'So maybe we're going in the right direction, but it's meant that drivers now, much more, do what they're told by the team. Because they have to in some ways, because the team's managing every aspect of their performance. Whereas you were left to your own devices. When I started driving with Williams, there wasn't a trainer, there wasn't anybody there making sure I was going home and doing my training. And when Frank wanted me to do some promotional event, I said, "I don't mind doing it, but can I make sure there's a gym in the hotel where I go, because I've got to keep fit," and he thought I was joking. He thought I was trying to kid him that I was keeping fit. That's because the generation before me did

Hill pictured towards the end of his Grand Prix career. Note the use of his famously intense eyes on his fireproof top. (Motorsport Images)

damn all. They probably did something, but they didn't do anything like the training that these guys do.'

Well, Stirling used to reckon he was amazingly fit because he was racing every weekend. And he also did some water skiing. But that's about it.
'I've seen a picture of Dad and Jim Clark down in Australia, with their shirts off, and they looked so unfit. They did not have any physique at all. My dad was probably still undernourished from the war. But now, if you see a picture of a guy, he's really toned. They're right up there with the top athletes and their diet is different.

'I often thought Dad did well at Monaco because he had stamina because he was an oarsman. That was the longest, toughest race, so you had to concentrate, you had to be fit. So it's possible that with my dad his advantage was his fitness – aerobic fitness, cardiovascular fitness.

'Then you got to the Nigel Mansell era, and you really needed to be strong. Nigel was enormously powerful and could hang on to the car. I drove that same car he'd raced, the active car. And believe me, it was a big old heavy thing to muscle around.'

So back to sort of pre-war days.
'Maybe, yeah, but they didn't have the g-load. The steering wheel might have been heavy and the gear change, and the brakes might have been heavy, but we used to be pulling quite a few g on top of that. But when you saw Nigel jump out of the car, he really was exhausted. He put a bit of a dramatic slant on it as well, but it was exhausting.'

I can remember reading, as a child, so probably in the late 1950s or early '60s, that a Grand Prix was said to be the equivalent of going 12 rounds in a heavyweight boxing match.
'Yeah, probably. It really was quite gruelling. But Michael Schumacher brought it to another level. He could do a whole Grand Prix in Malaysia and jump out with not a bead of sweat on him. I don't think I coped that well with the heat of the race. In Magny Cours he just slaughtered us, but my drink bottle broke. I remember coming on the

During the 1996 season, Hill went up against teammate Jacques Villeneuve for the World Championship. This is Silverstone, where Villeneuve came out on top. (Motorsport Images)

radio and saying, "I need a drink. When I come in for my pit stop, give me some water."

'I stopped and Patrick Head came out with a jug of water and I opened my mouth and he poured it down my neck [much laughter]! What the bloody hell? Before I had a chance to complain about that, I had to go again so I never got a drink. And it was 40 degrees then; it was ridiculous. They were spraying the crowd down with hoses at the start of the race. It was really very hot. Michael Schumacher just jumped out without even a bead of sweat on him.'

Who was the best teammate you had?
'In terms of having the best relationship, in Formula One, in my first team it was Eric van de Poele. He was a lovely guy, but we only really did half a season and then I was straight in with Alain Prost and Nigel Mansell, and then Ayrton Senna. Alain was a perfect gentleman. Nigel was very supportive. And I never got to know Ayrton that much.

'So the next year the guy I had for a full season was DC [David Coulthard], who I found a little bit testy. A little bit too chirpy for my liking [laughing]. I was a bit miffed that I had someone else in the team, to be honest, that I had to race against and then they got Jacques Villeneuve in. He was a kind of a keen puppy, you know, in a very confident [way] and attempted to establish his place in the team. But we got on really well: he was absolutely direct and very sporting, and I think we had a good relationship considering we were both fighting for the world title.

'I would never expect him to do anything underhand. There was the usual competitiveness for resources, let's say, within a team, but I never got the sense that he was going to try and do something unsporting in any way. I don't think Williams would have done that anyway. So we both got a fair crack at the Championship. It was tragic that his wheel fell off in Japan but there you go!'

Was there anyone who you would avoid going wheel-to-wheel with in a race?
'Not the really great drivers. I wouldn't have a problem with that. Michael was famously aggressive. If you look at what he did to me

and then compare it to what goes on today, it wasn't that out of order, frankly. It looked it at the time. It was considered to be pushing the boundaries a bit, but actually now I would say, looking back at it, it wasn't that unusual by today's standards. There were one or two things that he probably wouldn't get away with today and the stewards would probably penalise him for. By and large, he wasn't that bad.

'The worst ones are the guys who are inexperienced, and they just don't have the awareness, you know. So going wheel-to-wheel with someone who's slightly irrational is more scary than somebody who's very competitive. Because, generally, the people who are very competitive absolutely know what they're doing, and where you are, and what to expect. So it's the red-mist guys you need to watch out for.'

Talking of red mist, who do you think was the bravest?
'The bravest was Nigel.'

I thought you might say that!
'I think that you have to say what Ayrton did, getting in the car in Imola [after Roland Ratzenberger's fatal accident during practice in 1994], was probably an act of supreme bravery. I think he was in no doubt that what he did was potentially fatal. He didn't just get in the car and drive that weekend. He gave it more at Imola, I think, because he was determined not to be intimidated by the sport. So that was an act of heroism.

'But Nigel, I would say, and that is borne out by seeing him in Indy. Alonso is pretty brave too. They've all got a very high level of courage but Nigel was awesome. The confidence he had in his own ability and his own indestructibility was quite impressive.'

This is a rather corny question, but what do you think made the great ones great?
'Now, what is a great driver? Let's first define that. There are drivers who win a bit, and come and go. I would say I fit probably in that: I did very well, but I'm not in the great category. I didn't dominate an era. I popped up and was there for a bit, but I didn't actually dominate for any length of time. Whereas my dad was a front-runner throughout the 1960s, dominated Monaco, won half the Monaco Grand Prix races in the 1960s. He also won the two other major events in the sport – Indy and Le Mans – and drove and raced in everything.

'So this versatility and his courage and adaptability to different things was a mark of greatness. I put him in that category. And Moss as well with the Mille Miglia – what they did at other places, not just in the Formula One arena.'

Stirling rallying…
'Yep. And then being the spokesperson or the ambassador for their sports thereafter, I think cemented their place in that Pantheon. You know, I think Stirling was always a person everyone went to for some insight. He was very intelligent, very thoughtful and very direct with his views. He didn't hold back. If he thought something was wrong, he'd say so. So as individuals, they're very impressive people. I mean, Fangio clearly was in that category, too. And Senna. You have to say Senna was a great because of his recognition that there was something beyond just driving a racing car in circles. That was important. And I think he knew he was driving for a reason. It wasn't just to win. I mean, he had, I would say, his failings: it can't always be about one person.

'So, great drivers: just technically and as driving artists, I think you have to have Prost and Stewart in that category. They made it look easy. Probably Moss and Fangio in that bracket as well – the guys who make it look easy. And Hamilton as well. He gets in the car, usually on a Friday, and he's scrappy as hell, you know. It's like he hasn't really got his mind into being a racing driver again. And then over the weekend, he just suddenly starts to float, the focus comes in and then he's like a laser. He's just incredible. And his ability to turn up the wick and extract ultimately high performance levels out of himself, seemingly at will, is extraordinary. He has his dips, when his mind goes and he feels a bit negative and then you have the engineer on the radio, Pete Bonnington, saying, "Calm down, we're okay. Just keep at it." Sure enough, he dishes out some ridiculous performance. And he wins the race. He's got that ability.

'Of course, you can't discount Alonso, as I mentioned before, and Michael Schumacher. Again, they were formidable competitors. And they didn't just dominate the other drivers; they dominated the whole sport. That's the difference. Everybody in the paddock, all of the guys who run teams, the mechanics, journalists, they all know these guys are the ones.'

How do you think Schumacher and Senna compared? It was such a shame they didn't really overlap for very long.
'The difference was this, I think: Senna let his emotions get the better of him. In a way he drove angry, it seemed to me, and I don't think Michael drove angry. I think Michael was clinical. He always seemed to have a clear head – he was bloody fast. That's what I think the difference was. Michael, very rarely did you see him revved up. When he crashed into the back of David Coulthard at Spa, he was pretty… I think he was frightened, frankly. He'd had a big fright going into the back of a car he didn't expect to be there. And so that turns into anger, doesn't it?'

I think it is interesting that both had supreme ability, but both also did naughty things on track and could be underhand.
'I think Ayrton pushed the boundaries of what was sporting – if you don't go for the gap, you're not a racing driver? Well, there's some gaps you don't go for, like going into the first corner at Suzuka [in 1990]. That looked like just an assassination attempt. I don't know if he ever regretted doing that, but it was not something that looked terribly good. And it was extremely dangerous for everyone else. But Michael, I think he took the view that you get away with what you can. And if you get caught and pay the price, maybe you come out ahead if you don't pay the price the other times. That's just a different philosophy, isn't it?

'If you go and do your tax, your accountant

Suzuka 1996: Schumacher congratulates Hill on becoming World Champion. (Motorsport Images)

will try and get you to pay as little tax as possible. It's up to the tax man to find out whether or not you're doing it right. That's one way of looking at it. The other way of looking at it is, "You're supposed to pay this amount of tax, and you should pay it [laughing]."

'So with sporting regulations, you can argue the toss over certain interpretations, and I think that Michael and Ross Brawn and co, they definitely did that. That's fair

> *'Michael was famously aggressive. If you look at what he did to me and then compare it to what goes on today, it wasn't that out of order, frankly.'*

enough, but hoping not to get caught, I think is going beyond, isn't it?'

I've always felt they tainted their reputations and they didn't need to.
'Moss didn't mince his words about what he thought about some drivers. And he'd use the C-word but his was a different era. That's a personal choice and it is very tempting to get that competitive advantage, but when you've already got a God-given competitive advantage, I don't see why you jeopardise all of that.'

However, Prost would be much more correct. Would that be right?
'Yeah, I would say so. I think he won using his guile and his ability, like Lauda did. Lauda probably taught Prost a thing or two. Both were fast, but they didn't over-extend what they had. They went to the edge, but only if it was absolutely necessary. Like Fangio said, "You win at the slowest possible speed". And I would say that's an intelligent driver.'

On outright speed, how would you think Senna and Prost compared? Was Senna actually quicker or not?
'I think Senna could be quicker but I think he took risks. And I think that that can only go on for so long. But that was his courage, really. He was able to literally put his faith in his instincts, his driving instincts. I think Prost probably lost enough friends that way. And Jackie [Stewart] and co, I think that they probably kept a bit in reserve and used it only on special occasions.'

How would you rate Mario Andretti?
'Another great; absolute versatility. And also someone who key people really wanted to have in their car, people like Colin Chapman, because he brought so much. And very few people have managed to come from the States and win. He loves the sport and he's a very lovely guy as well. I went to Indy and we met, and he did an interview with us and [was] very generous with his time to come and talk to us. He seemed very calm; he is a calm guy. You'd never know he was a racing driver, really [laughing]!'

Riccardo Patrese?
'Riccardo's another lovely guy. I took his drive [at Williams] so he's probably not enamoured of me. But he'd left, actually, to be honest, he'd left the team. He could be very quick but he couldn't put pressure on Nigel. Good support in the team, a race winner, a very quick driver.

'You're asking what it is that makes someone great. It's what they are prepared to do, how hard to push themselves, perhaps. He seemed to keep quite quiet in the background. It wasn't immediately obvious that he was fiercely competitive.'

Won quite a lot of Grands Prix, though. How about Derek Warwick?
'You'd put Derek in the same category as Nigel, wouldn't you? So you'd have to ask yourself, what happened there? Why did Nigel get through and Derek didn't? And I think sometimes it's just bad luck. Maybe he didn't get the right slot at the right time.

'I think he was well positioned to be able to do whatever Nigel did. It was the musical chairs that kind of caught him out. He got blocked by Senna from going to Lotus [for 1986], and it would have been fun to see how he coped.

'I think in some ways, you'd have to say that's a tick in the box, or that's an indication of how good Derek was that Ayrton didn't want him to go there.'

That was very unfortunate. Jean Alesi?
'Naturally gifted. Loved racing. He clearly loves going fast. He loved his driving but he probably loved Ferrari too much because I think he stayed too long. Sometimes people get in a place and it's a very nice place to be as a Ferrari driver, and he knew he could battle with Gerhard, but if you're going to make a name, you've got to be in a place where you can win races.

'Another charming guy but I don't think he was prepared to do the things that someone like Senna would do to get himself in the best machinery. I can't imagine Jean going up to Ron Dennis [of McLaren] and saying, "I want to drive your car."

'Maybe there's a comfort level that some drivers get to. There's no doubting his natural ability and when I won the Spa race [in 1998], he was third. It was wet and talent shines [in those conditions].

'He made his name at Monaco, talented in the wet, lovely guy, fast… Don't know what happened there. He should have been a Michael Schumacher, really. I don't know what happened.'

Did anybody particularly stand out in the wet? I guess Senna?
'I wasn't bad [laughing]. Obviously Hamilton is brilliant in the wet. Alesi, of course, Prost.'

Why were you good in the wet?
'I liked it when the car was moving around. Yeah, I just like that feeling and searching for grip, for the traction and throttle control. And I also think you're zoned in for much longer when it's wet. You cannot relax, even on the straight. So your mind needs to be sharp.

'It's a more transcendental experience, driving in the wet. It's much more "feel and visual". You rely on your instincts much more. When you go right back, all the really talented drivers were good in the wet, people like Jackie Stewart.'

Stirling used to indulge in a bit of psychology and, if it was raining, before the race he'd go round the paddock, rubbing his hands with glee, saying, 'Love it'.
'And also he said he used to chuck the car around to make it look like it was more slippery than it really was. If you've got that

much abundance of talent, then you can afford to do those things.'

You mentioned Gerhard Berger earlier on. He seemed quite a character and used to play tricks on Senna. Was he more laid back, perhaps, than the rest?
'A couple of quotes from Gerhard: he said that he had an Austrian mindset and, in Austria, they live in very small valleys and that's their world. Whereas Ayrton he described as living in the world – he actually saw the whole of the moon rather than just a slice of Austria. I think that's Gerhard. He enjoyed life.

'He did say afterwards that he probably should have had a manager and it's interesting, I think, that he liked to be in charge of his own space. Maybe someone like Gerhard was too business-minded for most team bosses. Probably no team manager could take him under his wing because he was his own man really. And I think he got comfortable with Jean [Alesi] at Ferrari for too long. They had a good thing going there for a while.'

Who else stands out for you?
'We should mention Martin Donnelly. There was a talent where we never got to see its full potential. It was sad what happened, and also Johnny [Herbert] had extremely natural talent and was potentially at a Jim Clark level of ability.

'We haven't mentioned Jim Clark. Everything we have said [about the greats] applies to Jim – a modest, quiet person who really just had this incredible ability. He looked to me as if he was bewildered that anyone else would find it difficult. It was poetry in motion really, watching Jim Clark drive. So Johnny lost out, I think we lost the best of Johnny when he damaged his ankles. But he was one of those really gifted drivers. He still is a great, gifted driver – he hasn't given up.

'Mika Häkkinen. We talked about bravery. To have your head smacked open and then come back, the way he did, I think he was extremely courageous. And blindingly fast. I think Michael Schumacher was more intimidated by him than anyone else. I think he was probably the only person that intimidated him. So speed wasn't in question, but really astonishing to cope with what he went through and make his comeback. So, bravery? Right up there.'

How did you rate David Coulthard?
'I think David had a lot of natural ability, but his head seemed to be in different places. That was my assessment of David. I mean, he could be blindingly brilliant. But then, suddenly, he dropped the ball, it seemed to me. I'm not sure whether it was concentration or what it was, but he was a Grand Prix winner – he won Monaco twice – so the talent is all there but just, I think, slightly fragile on the concentration.'

How about Eddie Irvine?
'He's a legend, by his own admission [laughing], and has got a way about him which can make you feel you want to be rude back to him [more laughter]. He can be a little bit annoying personality-wise, but, again, great ability, no doubting the ability. But I think that he probably got people's backs up along the way.

'Interesting character, obviously very bright. He's made a lot of money since he stopped. I think he tried to suggest that he was a dilettante: he could come and do a bit of racing when he felt like it for Ferrari. But actually, I think, deep down, it was much more important to him than that. He's probably got some interesting stories to tell about Michael Schumacher.'

Any final thoughts in conclusion?
'The F1 experience is everyone's dream. Such a lot of hope is invested in it. And it puts every single driver through the mill dealing with the reality of what's involved. Very few people are able to put their feet down on solid ground. It's not a place you can just relax in at all. You're tested. So as a challenge, you can do other forms of motorsport, but nothing's quite like F1 for finding you out. I do respect all the drivers who've taken that challenge, and some I respect more than others because they've overcome it and managed to have longevity.

'The dream is to get to the point where you're wanted year on year [laughing]. But I was lucky to get my, what, seven years in F1. So it wasn't too bad.' ▰

Hill leads Michael Schumacher at a wet Spa-Francorchamps in 1998. He'd go on to win – the last of his 22 Grand Prix victories, and Jordan's first. (Motorsport Images)

MARIO ANDRETTI

Interviewed by **PETER WINDSOR**

MARIO ANDRETTI (USA)
Born 28 February 1940

Italian-born American Mario Andretti is perhaps the only serious rival to Stirling Moss's title of the most versatile racing driver of all time. Andretti won in Formula One, IndyCar, the World Sports Car Championship and NASCAR, and is the only driver ever to have won the Indianapolis 500, the Daytona 500 and the Formula One World Championship. In Grand Prix terms he remains most closely associated with Lotus, for which he took pole position at his debut race – the 1968 United States GP. Having rejoined the team in 1976, he helped to develop the ground-effect technology that delivered the World Championship two years later. Andretti raced full-time into the mid-1990s, and made his final appearance at Le Mans – one of very few major races to elude him – in 2000.

Andretti leads Lotus teammate Ronnie Peterson at the Dutch GP in 1978 – the year Andretti became World Champion. (Motorsport Images)

'**WHEN YOU REFLECT** upon the individuals with whom you rubbed elbows through the decades, it's inevitable that you're going to leave out some very important people. So the bottom line is this: I've been so blessed to have had opportunities to do my job alongside some of the best drivers the world will ever know.

'It starts from the beginning, from even when I first raced Modified stock cars. Who was the guy? A Pennsylvanian Dutchman called "Boopsie" Arner. He was just riding the rim with those things and that was it: he was the guy I had to beat.

'Then, when I got into three-quarter and full-size midgets, the kings were Len Duncan and Dutch Schaefer – individuals who historically are the icons of midget racing. I battled with them and they made a better driver of me, because I was trying to emulate them. I had so much reverence for them.

'Then you move onto sprint cars and the friendships I had with Jud Larson, AJ Foyt, Don Branson and Roger McCluskey – the top drivers of the day when I was trying to break in. I had maximum respect. I revered these people. How could they do it? You watch and you learn. When I was qualifying a sprint car on a dirt track somewhere and I was going after Don Branson, wherever he went that's where I was going to go. You relied on their ability and their knowledge and you figured that, if you were going to beat him, you had at least to do what they were doing and then try to do it better.

'Then in stock cars – NASCAR – you had Curtis Turner, Fred Lorenzen, Richard Petty, Dave Pearson. These were the icons who made the noise and when I had my day that's who I had to beat.

'Who were the kings when I got into F1? Jackie Stewart, Graham Hill, Jochen Rindt – people like that. It seems like every decade provided someone to look up to and to have the ultimate respect for. They were the yardsticks. They were the ones who set the stage on which you would bring the results you'd dreamt about.

'And not only did you respect all these people – you hoped that you were going to earn their respect as well. You always strive for that. For me, it was always extremely important not to be looked at as an idiot, just trying to get things done. I just wanted to feel that they had at least one-tenth of the respect for me that I felt for them.

'That's really the way I've gone through my career. I've always remembered that there's always someone out there better than you.

'I remember qualifying for the US GP at Watkins Glen in 1978. There was one corner where I had a specific issue – the right-hander after the 'boot' section at the end of the back straight. It's an easy enough corner, slightly downhill, but I had some issues there because you had to set up the car for the next corner.

'Then I followed Alan Jones through there – he was in the Williams FW06. I watched his line through there – he was running a much later apex, which initially didn't seem natural to me, but suddenly it all made sense. I did what he did on that corner and I put the car on pole. So there's always somebody who does something better than you and when you try to learn from that, then that's when

you move forwards. As soon as someone mentions Alan Jones to me, I always think of that corner at Watkins Glen. On my own, I couldn't make myself do that late apex. When I saw what Alan was doing, it all fell into place.

'But of course some drivers touch your soul as well. And the driver who did this for me was Dan Gurney. Why Dan? Because I'm in a midget car at Hatfield, Pennsylvania, ready to try to go out and try to win my third feature race of the day for the Mataka Brothers, and who am I thinking about? I'm thinking about Dan Gurney, who has just landed, with the help of Frank Arciero, a Ferrari drive in F1. Because Dan went to F1 when I was still in the dreaming stage, and because he was an American, I always identified with Dan. He was incredible. He had such a gentle demeanour and yet he was such a fierce competitor.

'Later, when we did the USAC road races, it was basically between Dan and me. It was pure racing. A pure battle. There was something about this man, and there was always a friendly hello every time I saw him. I used to say, "Hey, Champ!" It was Dan and his wife, Evi. There was something very warm between us – and there still is, by the way, with Evi.

'These were precious times and they have never gone away. You think about them immediately when you think of something worthwhile. There were others – but for some reason Dan left a real mark. Parnelli Jones was another one. Foyt too.

'In terms of teammates, I had very special friendships with both Gunnar Nilsson and Ronnie Peterson. With most teammates you don't have that really friendly, let's-meet-off-track-with-the-families relationship – or let's raise hell together – but with Gunnar and Ronnie it was different. We had that. Dee Ann, my wife, was very friendly with Ronnie and Barbro, so we spent some time together as a family. That made it very special.

'And then there were the drivers who inspired me right from the start. In my tender teenage years, Alberto Ascari was the guy. It was the early 1950s in Italy. Ferrari were winning everything with Ascari. He was the guy who started it all for me, who developed for me and my brother Aldo this desire to go motor racing.

'I always had this thing in the back of my

Andretti (second left) with Jochen Rindt, Colin Chapman and Graham Hill at the 1969 South African Grand Prix, and (right) in the gorgeous little Ferrari 312 PB that he shared with Jacky Ickx at Watkins Glen in 1971. (Motorsport Images)

mind that somehow, some day, F1 would have to be a part of my career. And lo and behold, there I was in 1965, in my rookie year at Indy, in the pit lane with Colin Chapman and Jimmy Clark. And in those days you were at Indy forever, so in my office on my special wall, in a special place, there's the picture of Jimmy and I just chatting during practice. And then with Colin, I just wanted to meet him and talk to him as much as possible.

'I had a good race in '65, finishing third and winning Rookie of the Year, so when we came to say our goodbyes after the banquet, there was Jimmy, the race winner, and there was me, also with a trophy, so I said to Colin, "Someday I would like to do Formula One."

'Colin replied, quickly: "Mario, when you think you're ready, call me. I'll have a car for you."

'Can you imagine that? Someone like Colin Chapman saying that? What it did do, immediately, is start me lobbying USAC like crazy for more road races. The only race I won in '65 was the first road race they held at Indianapolis Raceway Park. That's how things just started to come together. Precious times. Key moments in my life.

'Later, in 1969, I had the dubious honour of being the first driver ever to be kissed on a podium by a man. By Andy Granatelli, of course – my team owner, complete with garlic breath. But Andy certainly has a place in my heart. He was bigger than life in so many ways – a showman but with a very tender heart. I derived so much satisfaction in winning at Indy that year – not so much for myself but because I knew how badly Andy wanted to win at Indy. That's where we didn't always see eye-to-eye because to me Indy was just another race. Andy didn't care about anything else, but I did. For me, every race was important.

'Anyway, he always felt that he had to be thinking outside the box in order to win at Indy but in '69, after we crashed the four-wheel-drive Lotus in practice when something broke, we had to start the race with just the back-up Hawk – the car we never planned to race. And we won with it – with a good, basic race car created by Clint Brawner around a Brabham chassis. When I crossed the finish line, the first thing that came to mind was the look on Andy's face. I just cracked up – as did he.'

JACKIE STEWART

Interviewed by **PHILIP PORTER**

SIR JACKIE STEWART (GB)
Born 11 June 1939

Stewart's family ran a garage in Dumbarton and his brother Jimmy was a successful racing driver with the Ecurie Ecosse team. A talented shot, Jackie narrowly missed out on competing at the 1960 Olympic Games, before turning his attention full-time to motor racing. In 1964, he drove for Ken Tyrrell in Formula Three, marking the beginning of a long and successful association between the two men. Stewart made his Formula One debut in 1965 with BRM and won that year's Italian Grand Prix – the first of his then-record 27 victories at the highest level. He went on to win three World Championships, and following the death of Jim Clark in 1968, he was Formula One's acknowledged benchmark, also leading a campaign that helped to change the sport's often-woeful attitude to safety.

Who was your favourite teammate?
'François Cevert, certainly. He came as a puppy, really, not having driven in Formula One. And Ken Tyrrell was a wonderful man for developing young drivers, of any age actually, because he did a good job for Surtees as well when he moved from bikes to cars. I was part of making the choice of François Cevert coming over to Tyrrell with Elf, of course, who we were with at that time, and he was like a sponge. He just wanted to know everything. And I told him everything. I never held anything back. We had just a great relationship, which sadly, of course, ended in tears at Watkins Glen.'

For you, was Jim Clark the best?
'I think probably Fangio was the best of all time, in my opinion. But that, of course, goes back a long way. Whereas, in my window of time, in my opinion, second to none was Jim Clark. I would put him second, in fact, to Fangio. Above everybody else, above Schumacher, above Lewis Hamilton, above anyone else. Jim Clark drove so smoothly. Colin Chapman made very fragile cars, and there were many times components that weren't what I would describe as the very strongest or robust. Jim Clark didn't have many mechanical failures because he drove so smoothly.

'You know, I learned so much from Jim because we were Scots and we shared an apartment down in London belonging to Sir John Whitmore. So we spent a lot of time together, travelling, holidaying. He was never one to give you information, but you could take information from his driving. He was quite shy about discussing his braking distances or anything – he would never give me any of those. In a funny sort of way, it was a compliment. If he wasn't giving me the braking distances, he was slightly concerned that I might be getting a little closer.

'But to follow him, and the soft manner in which he drove, I learned so much. Actually, I [also] learned from my shooting before my racing because the mind management in shooting was very important – you couldn't afford to miss a target because you never got it back. Whereas in motor racing you can make a mistake in any corner but regain that error. So I learned a lot from that about smoothness.

'My brother, Jimmy Stewart, was a good racing driver and he was a smooth road driver. I was eight years younger than my brother, so I learned a lot from just driving road cars smoothly and, when I started to drive racing cars, I obviously did the same thing. Jim Clark only had two big accidents: one at Brands Hatch and the other one of course took his life. But so many other people were killed in Lotuses in Formula One, for example, or Formula Two because Chapman's cars were fragile, whereas Jimmy drove so smoothly.

'When you take your foot off the gas pedal, you just don't take it off, you caress it off, and you caress the brake pedal, and you do the same with the steering. So I learned a lot of that from driving for Ecurie Ecosse and my early experience. But Formula One is more demanding and therefore seeing Jimmy drive like that made me develop my driving.

'I have always said there are eight elements to a corner. To begin with there might only have been three: braking, the corner itself and accelerating. I broke that into eight different motions and that was smoothness: you don't come off the gas pedal fast, you come off it gently so it doesn't upset the car; you don't get on the brake pedal hard because it upsets the car; you don't put the steering angle in too fast or it upsets a car; you don't put the gas pedal on too hard as it upsets the car... So, there's eight different items. It was learning to do that at every corner – fast corners, slow corners – and that's why I think I got the number of Grand Prix victories I did.

'The March was pretty awful; the Matra was good. The BRM was good and from the BRM we went to the Matra, but from the Matra we had to go to the March, which was not an easy car to drive. It was a bit of a journeyman's car. It wasn't a sophisticated car because they put it together so quickly. I mean, they did a great job and we won a Grand Prix with it, but it wasn't fun to drive

Stewart holding off Clark – from whom he learnt so much – *en route* to his first Grand Prix win, Monza 1965. (Motorsport Images)

Master and pupil: Cevert was 'like a sponge' when he joined Stewart at Tyrrell, and they became close friends. (Motorsport Images)

it. The Matra was beautiful to drive because it was so beautifully engineered. The Matra people were very good: their aerospace technology was terrific, the attention to detail very strong and our engineers were very good, our team of Ken Tyrrell's people. The Tyrrell was more difficult to drive.

'But Jim Clark, for me, was the epitome of driving during my whole career — smooth in, exit perfect. I followed his manner of driving as best I could, and François therefore learned the same way. At the end, François was absolutely ready to be number one.

'I mean, I was always going to retire at the end of the [1973] season, but nobody knew it outside of Ken Tyrrell and Walter Hayes, and John Wardell, actually, of Ford Motor Company. Sadly, François never knew that he was going to be the number-one driver and Ferrari had approached him. So I was sad that I hadn't let them know that, but on the other hand it was right for me not to talk about retiring.'

How about Graham Hill?
'A very unusual driver, a more mechanical driver than Jimmy was. I learned a lot from him, and he was a wonderful entrée into Formula One for me. He never didn't give me an answer if I wanted to know something about a set-up or a corner or, you know, gear ratios or anything where he could easily have avoided answering because I was quite competitive right away. And I finished, what was it, third in the World Championship in my first year, won a Grand Prix and finished quite well.

'[That year] I could have gone to Cooper, I could have gone to Lotus with Jim Clark. But I chose to go to BRM because I thought it would be a more thorough apprenticeship, I thought I would get more testing. I saw Graham as a good man to understudy, because Jim Clark was such a huge natural talent that he just got into a racing car and made it happen. Graham got into a racing car and worked at it, as a driver and as an engineer and an analyst. He noted everything. Everything was in an old book: spring rates, gear ratios, steering ratios, everything. He wasn't a Jim Clark, but he was a good engineer-driver. He went about his business in such a thorough and disciplined fashion.

'Graham could easily have been less helpful towards me. And he wasn't. And so it was a lovely family as well. Because I had a family and Damon was a wee boy at that time and his two sisters were girls, and I used to spend time with them. When I used to go down and stay with Graham in the early days, I would come down from Scotland and we were testing, always at Snetterton. So I would stay overnight, two or three nights with the Hills.'

Always a cerebral driver, Stewart remains a perceptive observer of Formula One. (Michael Cole)

What about John Surtees?
'I never thought of him as a great driver. I think he was a journeyman driver. I never really got to know John Surtees. I drove in his team for two or three races with the Lola, once in Can-Am, I think, and the other in England — Brands Hatch and places like that. He never became what I would call comfortable with the Formula One fraternity. He was his own man. And he never seemed to quite get on as well with engineers and mechanics as Graham would have done, or Jim would have done, or maybe I would have done. But he was very focused, very committed and really wanted to do the job.

'I think he was a better bike racer than he was a Grand Prix World Champion. Driving for Ferrari at that time helped because the Ferrari was a very good car. He was a good driver, there's no doubt, but not of the same calibre as Jim, for example.'

Could we discuss Jochen Rindt?
'Jochen was a different kettle of fish altogether. And again, as much of a friend as Jimmy was, because Nina and Helen got on very well and they lived very close by us. He was overly ambitious to begin with and overdrove most of the time. You could do that with a Formula Two car, but you couldn't do it with a Formula One car.

'Therefore it took him quite a long time to be successful in Formula One. He drove for Brabham, and he drove for Cooper, and never really got it done. When he drove for Chapman, however, the [Lotus] 49 was an amazing car, by far the best car on the track at that time. He was a good friend of Jimmy's, as well. And I'm sure he came of age, by learning not to drive fast, you know, not to have to drive fast to get a car to go fast. And in the end, he was very good.

'In Formula Two, he was fast and won more races than I did in Formula Two, and probably more races than Jimmy did in Formula Two, but he was always sideways, you know, there was much opposite lock and you can play with a Formula Two car. So different. A different animal altogether than Formula One. And in Formula One, he overdrove. Whereas by the time he got to Lotus, he wasn't overdriving. But by that time, he started to become pretty

knowledgeable about the sport with regard to engineering, but he was never a happy man at Lotus. I'm sure he would have retired after his World Championship [in 1970], because we talked about it. I mean, we lived 400 metres away from each other. And Nina and Helen are still best friends. We spent a lot of time together.

'He was fourth to me in '69 [in the World Championship] when I had the Matra, and one of the best races I've ever had in my life was with Jochen at Silverstone for the British Grand Prix, which I won but we passed each other over 30 times. But we always passed each other by telling each other where to pass because we were such good friends, because you were going to pass going down Hangar Straight. But if you moved over and let the guy through, you didn't slow up. And the same with Abbey Curve. You could overtake from Abbey to Woodcote, but we would point to each other where we should pass.

'The records will not show that there were 30 lead changes because the lead change was [only registered] at Woodcote. But we'd be changing on Hangar Straight going into Stowe. And we would change going into Woodcote from Abbey Curve because of the slipstream but we never did it to bother each other. They were always easy overtakes, because I'd back off or he would back off. So why f**k him up, pardon my French, because it would have slowed us both down.

'We lapped the whole field. There was nobody even close to us. But that was two people who knew each other intimately, weren't biting each other and could trust each other. In fact, the last time I passed him, his rear wing endplate and the wing got loose and was bouncing off the tyre. Now, I could see that but he couldn't see it. So when I passed him going into Stowe, like we were doing, I pointed to his right-rear wheel, because there was going to be a big shunt if he wasn't careful. In fact, it did fall off and he went in. And then for some reason the car didn't have enough fuel, by which time I was way ahead. But we lapped the whole field in that race, one of the best I've ever had, and one of the most enjoyable.

'So he was a very good friend, tough guy, but a very good friend. Also, Bernie [Ecclestone] was very into him. And he to Bernie, I'm sure. He was going to retire at the end of the season when sadly he died. I'm sure he would have worked with Bernie on something.'

How did you rate Jack Brabham?

'I never thought he was a smooth driver, but he was a very good driver. And, of course, the only man to be World Champion in his own car in Formula One. He would use the edge of the road regularly to knock stones and God knows what up at you, and you got blood everywhere because in those days, we had open helmets and things like that. And he would just do it.

'In Formula Two, he had the Honda engine. None of us could really beat the Honda engine but we would always be racing him – he and Denny Hulme. Clearly, he was a good driver but I wouldn't have said he was a great driver. Stirling Moss and Jim Clark were very smooth, clean drivers, really smooth. Graham wasn't that but never wild. Jack was quite wild; there was a lot of opposite lock. And he'd sometimes forget to change gear. You were up his backside, you could hear the engine revving, and then he would suddenly change gear.'

What about Mario Andretti?

'Very versatile: Indianapolis, NASCAR, Formula One, touring cars, endurance racing... a charming man. Very Italian-American, because he was very well mannered and very smooth, and I found him a very nice man to be racing with. And he was a good racer. I never felt uncomfortable, ever, racing with Mario Andretti so I respect him highly. He was a nice man to be with. He was a good friend to travel with and to hang out with. And of course, he's still here, which is a big advantage!'

How about Emerson Fittipaldi?

'Emerson, again, another gentleman, and colourful. We both had very long hair! There was a big competition as to who had the longest sideburns. We had a lovely picture taken of us. There was a photo of Muhammad Ali and one of the big boxers with their heads together. And we couldn't do it. We kept laughing. There is a picture but they've just snapped it before we ruined the picture again. We couldn't stop laughing.

'We would holiday together when we were at the height of our careers. Helen and I stayed in his house, like I stayed in Jimmy's house, like I stayed in Graham's house and they stayed in mine. So, Emerson was a really good racing driver and it was absolutely right he won World Championships. Of course, he was with Lotus but he carried the sport well. He started the whole Brazilian movement into Formula One with Nelson Piquet and so forth. All of the drivers from Brazil should be saying a big "thank you" [to Fittipaldi]. He was a great ambassador for Brazil.

'The other thing he did, which was very smart, was to get major multinationals and rich people in Brazil to support Formula One, and so forth, because he got many of the sponsorships. There was John Player and he had a lot to do with them coming in with money.

'He was very competitive. I lost a lot of races with him. Definitely. The Brazilian Grand Prix: that's one I never won, which I'm still annoyed about. He was first [in 1973] and I was second and he was well ahead of me. My Tyrrell at that time was a very difficult car to drive: it was a short-wheelbase car. The Lotus was a very good car to drive. Colin Chapman made very fast cars – they weren't always reliable, but they were quick. And Emerson took full advantage of that. He didn't do so well with his own team in his own car, obviously. But a great ambassador for the sport who still attends Grands Prix from time to time.

'Sadly, Jack is no longer with us [and] neither are Jochen, or John, or Graham or Jim. And I have to say of that era, I think there was a better line-up of talented drivers than I think there's ever been. Mike Spence was very good – a lot of very good drivers.'

Would you include Ronnie Peterson?

'Yeah, exactly. Oh, yes. I think it was the halcyon period of very good drivers. If you look back to those days and see the grids – Chris Amon was a top-line driver. Never quite had the right car at the right time, but a beautiful driver, smooth and immaculate, and no nonsense.'

On the ragged edge: Rindt leads Stewart during their famous battle at the 1969 British GP. (Motorsport Images)

TONY BROOKS

Interviewed by **PHILIP PORTER**

TONY BROOKS (GB)
Born 25 February 1932

Tony Brooks was one of the greatest racing drivers of his generation, winning six Grands Prix in a relatively short career – he retired at the end of 1961 at the age of just 29. He scored a historic win for Connaught at the 1955 Syracuse Grand Prix – the first victory for a British car at that level in more than 30 years – and in 1958 he won three times for Vanwall. It's a measure of his talent that those victories came at blue-riband races – the Belgian, German and Italian Grands Prix. He moved to Ferrari in 1959 and won twice more, finishing second to Jack Brabham in that year's World Championship. After a trying year with BRM in 1961, he retired to run his garage business.

'**DRIVERS CAN ONLY** be fairly compared who have competed in the same period – the 1950s, in this case. It was what I refer to as the "dangerous" period in Formula One, when the use of public roads was the first challenge and the 16-20 competing drivers the second. When a driver lost control of his car, how it finished up was in the lap of the gods, there being the choice of brick walls, telegraph poles/booth, or a ditch to flip it over a hedge into a field, etc.

'Fangio and Moss were the outstanding drivers in the period. I drove with or against both of them for seven years – four of them in the same Aston Martin team in the case of Moss – and during the 1950-'60 decade I won 50 per cent of the Grands Prix I finished, only Fangio, Moss and Ascari winning more Grands Prix in the decade. I am well qualified to make a comparison!

'Despite Moss's all-round ability, Fangio was the greater driver, the former having some basic weaknesses which are explained [below]. These are the only drivers I am prepared to give clearly earned praise to, because there are no others racing in circumstances I would be prepared to consider comparable.'

The following extract is taken from the book *Poetry in Motion* by Tony Brooks with his kind permission...

'[Juan Manuel Fangio] was the most natural driver at the time, so good that he could produce outstanding performances without exceeding his personal safety margins. His many attributes included great mental strength, the ability to concentrate 100 per cent for the whole of a race, remarkable anticipation and judgment, with exceptional eyesight, and sensitivity in his hands, feet and the seat of his pants. He was never impetuous at the start of a race, taking time to size up the situation, and drove very intelligently, always one step ahead, believing that the aim of the game was to win the race at the lowest possible speed. What gave him his edge was the combination of all these gifts, each one possessed to a high degree, making him a complete driver, the result being unique.

'In his book with Roberto Carozzo, *My Racing Life*, Fangio states: "As in all things, you need good organisation in order to win. I have never been a spectacular racer, I never went into it as a form of escapism. I was always out to win, if this was at all possible. If there was some crazy guy around, I let him overtake, and then tried to follow him, never letting him get out of sight… I repeat: a lot of people would have beaten me if they had followed me. They lost because they overtook me."

'As an example of his last remark he referred to Ascari and Moss in the 1954 Italian Grand Prix at Monza, where Fangio had problems with his streamlined Mercedes-Benz running on only seven cylinders and he was saving his brakes: "Suddenly, along came Moss and passed both of us [Ascari and Fangio]. Then Ascari went off in pursuit of the Englishman's Maserati. First Ascari broke down, and then Moss, not far from the finish, while I was struggling with the streamlined Mercedes-Benz which was proving fairly hard to handle."

'He further commented: "Ascari and Moss shouldn't have driven that race as they did… Moss did himself out of a victory by trying to go faster and faster when he had a lead of half a lap. He ended up with a broken-down Maserati, and I won, not exactly deservingly."

'His attributes were not just confined to driving technique and racecraft. He was recognised not only as the best driver but as the fairest. I never heard a single complaint about his behaviour in or out of the cockpit and few indeed are the World Champions about whom this could be said, an outstanding ambassador for the sport. He was extremely modest, but when he

Brooks's neutral Vanwall battles Fangio's drifting Maserati at the 1957 Italian GP. He describes the great Argentine as 'the complete driver'. (Motorsport Images)

entered a room it went quiet, his persona creating a reaction similar to that afforded to royalty. He commanded awe.'

***

'Thank goodness Stirling Moss survived. He was a truly great driver, the best all-rounder, driving everything outstandingly well, including rally cars. He was the best in sports cars and should have won the F1 Drivers' World Championship several times, as previously mentioned.

'[I have] described the characteristics I believe made Fangio the great driver he was and the physical ones applied equally to Stirling, who was also a great natural driver, yet I believe he had to push himself just that fraction harder than Fangio, to psych himself up on occasions, as evidenced by the time he had to keep staring at the instruments instead of the road ahead to take a corner flat at Syracuse. He continued to hone his driving and I believe gained some speed in his later years to justify the mantle he inherited from Fangio.

'It was in strategy and tactics that the two seemed to differ, Fangio believing that the object was not to drive faster than was necessary to win the race, taking time to weigh up every situation, whereas Stirling would go like a bat out of hell from the drop of the flag and frequently seemed determined to demonstrate the extent of his superiority by winning by an unnecessarily large margin.

'The Championship eluded him because of what he did out of the car, not in it. He turned down an unbelievable offer from

Brooks adored the 1959 Ferrari 246, seen here in 'short nose' form at Monaco. He joined the Scuderia from Vanwall, where Moss (above) and Stuart Lewis-Evans were his teammates. (Motorsport Images)

Ferrari in 1952 and seemed addicted to what I have called "mechanical fiddling" with his "specials" in an effort to provide himself with a faster car than the opposition, or at least with an edge, whereas all he needed was a car as good as the opposition plus reliability.

'In 1955 and thereafter, he normally had a car on the pace, which I would have liked to have regularly enjoyed but didn't due to some poor decisions, my competitive cars being confined to my two years with Vanwall, one with Ferrari and four with Aston Martin. It was what Stirling did to produce a competitive car that was the problem. Sometimes it was a "mongrel" using an unreliable gearbox, other times a much-modified standard car, and sometimes it was indecision between two marques at the same meeting. Fangio thought as clearly out of the cockpit as he did in it, achieving five World Championships in four different factory cars.

'Stirling said the danger of motor racing gave him a kick and I suspect that initially he was not a wholehearted supporter of the drive to make motor racing much safer, started by Jackie Stewart, and probably even Jackie didn't anticipate that the sport could become as safe as it is today.'

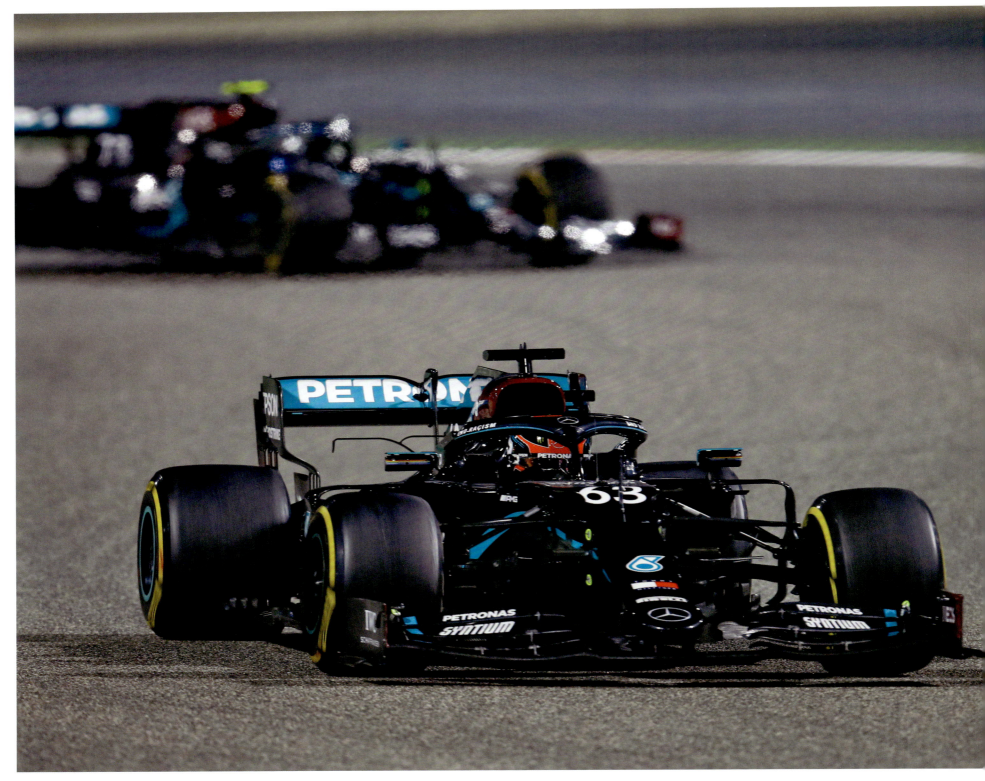

GEORGE RUSSELL

Interviewed by **DAVID TREMAYNE**

GEORGE RUSSELL (GB)
Born 15 February 1998

Russell started karting at the age of seven and graduated to cars in 2014, when he won the BRDC Formula 4 Championship. After two seasons in the European Formula Three Championship, Russell moved up to GP3 in 2017 and won the title, as he did the following year in GP2. That earned him a seat with the Williams Formula One team in 2019, and he claimed his first points-scoring finish in 2020. That year, he was also an impressive stand-in for Lewis Hamilton – who had tested positive for COVID-19 – at Mercedes for the Sakhir GP. In 2022, he will join Hamilton in the team full-time.

Of all the drivers you have raced against in your career, which one, or ones, stood out for you?

'His stats speak for themselves, but seeing and working with Lewis [Hamilton] during my time with Mercedes was very refreshing – to see that a guy on his level is not just relying on his talent but was really putting in the extra effort and hours to optimise his results. And that was almost a little bit of a reality check for me – that actually, to be the best, you need to work like crazy.'

Which driver has been the best teammate you've had?

'I really enjoyed racing and working with Robert Kubica. He was a great guy, great personality, very technically intelligent. And that taught me a lot, especially in my first year of racing – how to deal with the engineers, the team, how to make the car go faster. And again, it taught me that I do need to raise my game on the technical side of things and he helped me do so.'

Who was your most challenging teammate?

'In 2015, I raced in Formula Three and I was teammates with [Antonio] Giovinazzi. In the first half of that year, he was very, very competitive – all season, he was very competitive. But compared to myself, he was more competitive at the start of the year. And that made it very difficult for me because I wasn't used to being on the back foot. I probably learned more in that half-year of difficulty than I learned in the subsequent three years or so when I was winning, because dealing with success is easy. Dealing with disappointment is the hardest challenge.'

Which driver do you think is the best of all time, and why?

'I think Lewis is the best of all time purely because I know how fantastic the competition is these days and how hard he works. And obviously, the statistics speak for themselves.'

Which driver or teammate have you had the most fun with?

'I had a lot of fun with Alex Albon. He's a close friend of mine. Being on holiday together, we've probably got stories about each other that we probably wouldn't want shared – good stories, nothing too bad! But we know a lot about each other and have had a lot of fun along the way over the past five or six years.'

Who is the bravest driver that you've ever seen?

'Kevin Magnussen was pretty fearless. When he was on track, he pushed things properly to the boundaries. We all know how dangerous motorsport is and you've got to be pretty fearless and brave to do that. So, probably Magnussen.'

What was the biggest disappointment in your career?

'I guess the biggest disappointment was missing out on the victory in Bahrain last year [2020]. I've had a lot of tough moments throughout my career but definitely losing out on winning a Formula One Grand Prix was massive. Obviously, given the circumstances, it would have been very special. But to be honest, I probably wouldn't change it for anything and everything. Things happen for a reason. So let's hope there's a good reason after all for this.'

Russell in Bahrain in 2020, when he came so close to winning his first Grand Prix. (Motorsport Images)

ALLAN McNISH

Interviewed by **IAN WAGSTAFF**

ALLAN McNISH (GB)
Born 29 December 1969

McNish's early career was spent in single-seaters. He won the 1988 Formula Vauxhall Lotus Championship and was runner-up in the following year's British Formula Three Championship. He later competed in Formula 3000 and had a single season in Formula One with Toyota (2002), but he became far better known as one of the best sports car drivers of his generation. In a long career with Audi, McNish won the Le Mans 24 Hours three times, the Sebring 12 Hours four times, and the 2013 World Endurance Championship. He also won the American Le Mans Series three times before retiring in 2013.

McNish hustles the Audi R10 to victory in the Petit Le Mans race at Road Atlanta in 2006. (Motorsport Images)

Of all the drivers you raced against in your career, which one stood out in each decade?
'I think if I look back into the '80s, then it probably is a driver called Andrea Gilardi, who was [Junior] World Karting Champion in 1984 and 1985. That was at the time when I was doing what they called Junior International, and raced in the Championship in 1985 at Le Mans, on the Alain Prost circuit, and Andrea was fantastically quick. He won two World Championships but as well he was a suave Italian and looked to have everything at his feet.

'In that '85 Championship, Michael Schumacher finished second, I finished equal third. And there were a lot of very high-quality drivers as it turned out. So you know, Andrea was definitely the one that stood out for me in that decade.'

What happened to him?
'Well, two things happened to him, very unfortunately. After winning that Championship, he turned 16 and he had a little scooter. He was on his scooter and somebody knocked him off. He was static at the time but it broke his pelvis and [as a result] he lost a bit of momentum. He made his way to Formula 3000 but never with, I would say, the backing and the right teams. And so the momentum went out of his career very early on, and at the same time, very unfortunately, his father passed. I think his father was quite a driving force in terms of pushing things forward, as parents are, for every young kid looking to go from karting into cars.

'Andrea, funnily enough, is still involved because he works for the Audi Driving Experience in Italy. But very honestly, his talents were such that he should have been driving at the front of top-line grids in the world of car racing. A lost talent.

'In terms of the 1990s, I've got a wide variety of teammates to choose from. Mika Häkkinen was also in the Marlboro World Championship programme. Mika was my direct teammate in 1988 in Opel Lotus, when we were at Dragon Motorsport as two young kids. Also, Michael Schumacher, because I was the test reserve at Benetton at that time when he was making his way through in 1993-'94.

'But for me, the one I was directly involved with, I would actually say Laurent [Aïello]. It's easy to say Mika and it's easy to say Michael, but I was with Laurent in '91 at DAMS in Formula 3000. And then also in '98, when we won Le Mans together for the first time. Laurent was an exceptional natural talent. Very, very different mentality. Probably not cut out for corporate motor racing at all, but without question in karts, or whether it be in a 3000 car or touring car or a sports car, he had an adaptability and a capability to jump in and be blindingly fast, and to win in different types of touring cars, all around the world. That showed he was a special talent behind the wheel.'

Can you elaborate on what you mean by corporate motor racing?
'There was conforming to certain rules and there's conforming to your own rules, and Laurent definitely conformed to his own rules. A lot of drivers – Stirling, I think, was a little bit the same when you talk about that type of thing – they pushed against the trend, if you like. I think in the '80s and '90s, it was very much a corporate world.

'We have to remember there was major corporate sponsorship that was bringing drivers through racing programmes. It was the time of the double-breasted suit and the pleated trousers and the tassel shoes, and all of these sorts of things. That's when business was becoming a very big part of racing, driver/managers were becoming a very big part of racing, the corporate sponsorship, everything else was suddenly taking racing from [being] sponsorship on the side of a car to being an active part of the business of motor racing. And some people could absorb that part of it, and some people struggled.

'I've said to quite a few young drivers, nowadays probably 70 per cent of their job is outside the cockpit and 30 per cent is inside the cockpit. So if you want to make it, you've got to work harder outside the cockpit than you do inside the cockpit, in a way. That's normally not the thought process: if you're a fast driver and can deliver, then everything's gonna be okay. If you're an exceptional talent, like Laurent, that is the case – but the word "exceptional" in there, I think, probably defines the people that can get away with it. Your Kimi Räikkönens can get away with that dismissive attitude. And, you know, Jacques Villeneuve could get away with it, having one PR day in his contract, whereas, I would say, 99.9 per cent of racing drivers just wouldn't be hired.

'In the '80s and '90s, if you'd have turned up with a sports psychologist, you would have been taken back out of the paddock and your pass cancelled. Now it is deemed to be part of the development of a driver, and correctly so. I grew up in an era where you self-taught these things. I worked out what made me tick, or worked out what were my trigger points, good and bad, and worked out solutions for them. But that obviously took a lot of mistakes, and a lot of years to be able to do that. Whereas, you know, you can fast-track these things with trainers, such as for public speaking and that sort of thing.

'We were lucky, my era of drivers, especially Scottish drivers, that we had Jackie [Stewart], because Jackie was one of the benchmark step points in terms of that. Jackie was always there as, not just a guiding light, but also very much a guiding hand as well for us. I think that accelerated myself along and I saw it with Mika Häkkinen, actually, and Keke [Rosberg]. Keke was maybe a bit more of a maverick. But the way that it's structured in our junior careers with Marlboro and everything else tried to bring in that corporate side, always dressing with the correct clothing at the correct time, always making sure that you had a haircut before you went through your photoshoot. If you see some of my '80s photoshoots, clearly I didn't do that!'

How about the first decade of the 21st century?
'There's two that stand out for me. One of them is [Rinaldo] "Dindo" Capello, who was my longtime teammate through Audi, basically from the beginning to the end. There is also Mika Salo because Mika was my teammate at Toyota and it was the first

year for the team [in F1]. That was obviously a tough season for everybody: the car didn't develop, we were on the back foot a little bit and continually going towards the back of the grid. But he was always straight. He was always honest, brutally so sometimes. But at the same time, he was a good teammate, and always had a sense of humour.

'I actually gained a lot of respect for Mika Salo because it would have been very easy, with the experience he had in F1 – and also, he had the only engineer in the whole team that actually had experience of F1 – to be able to try to screw me over, but that wasn't his way at all. Having raced him in British Formula Three, I had known him since the 1980s and he actually went up in my estimation.

'But my driver of the 2000s has got to be "Dindo" Capello because, first of all, he became an extremely close friend but he was also a fantastically quick driver. When we first met, he had only really done touring cars in Italy. He had never really been outside Italy, he smoked like the Flying Scotsman, he was unfit, like you wouldn't believe – he couldn't run the length of himself without being out of puff. When aeroplanes were starting to ban smoking, he used to choose airlines by the ones that were still allowing it. And he didn't speak very much English at all. Not to say that's a problem but it certainly didn't help communications within the team. And he was, I would say, a little bit shy in a way. But underneath was one of the biggest dynamos that I ever came across in my career and one of the biggest transformations of a person, once you were able to peel back the layers.

'By the end of the 2000s, he spoke very good English. He had a tremendous, tremendous sense of humour. He was very much a people's person. He was the bond between Tom Kristensen and I, no question.

The works Porsche 911 GT1 of McNish, Laurent Aïello and Stéphane Ortelli *en route* to victory at Le Mans in 1998. (Motorsport Images)

And he was the bond within Audi. He was a lovable person to the point that I spent more time with "Dindo" in some years than I did with my wife. Our son used to say he was like daddy's second wife, you know, his other wife.

'But in terms of speed, he's done things with that sports car that I don't think I could ever have done. In Portland, we were qualifying and the tyres lasted one lap. We were struggling badly with the set-up in free practice [so] we took the sister car set-up. Emanuele Pirro was with us at the time and it was in 2000, so we were against the BMW with JJ Lehto, and Panoz with [David] Brabham and [Jan] Magnussen.

'"Dindo" messed up the lap completely, and we were, like, four or five tenths off the pace. He was still going around and I'm thinking we're finished. We're fourth or fifth on the grid. All we're doing is using a tyre life for the race. I'm starting the race and that's my set of tyres! I kind of switched off; I'd gone off the pit wall. I heard a little bit of shouting and turned round – and he's just stuck it on pole by a tenth and a half. I asked him how he did it and he said, "I don't know – I just threw it around and got the time out of it." He was able to do these things without necessarily being able to compute how he did it at the beginning, but later through his career he understood exactly how to do it.

'He won the Monza Rally when there were rally drivers [competing] so it wasn't an amateur thing. He won the Rally of Monza several times. He could jump into a touring car and be fast, a sports car, whatever it was. The interesting thing about "Dindo" is that he's now, I think, the second or third biggest Audi dealer in Italy. He's got a massively direct and clever business sense. But without question, for me, "Dindo" is the man of the 2000s.'

And finally your last decade?

'Well, I was only racing for three years because I retired in 2013. I have to say Tom [Kristensen] because we had quite a lot of success but also endured pain in terms of races that got away, especially at Le Mans. And 2013 at Le Mans was a very, very tough year, because the weather was just so inconsistent. I don't think I did two laps in the full 24 hours with the same weather conditions, so you're always living right on the edge.

'It was a year when we had the speed but not an advantage, so we were always trying to pull off a stroke against the opposition. It was a year where we were on average about 25 or 30 seconds ahead of the Toyota in changing conditions when you were on slicks on a damp circuit. It was a really tough race mentally more than physically.

'And it was the year where Allan Simonsen was killed at the beginning of the race. From any racing driver's point of view, that was a shock. We know these things can happen; we're very, very aware of it. And we protect ourselves as much as we can, but we know that can happen. But I think for the Danish driver, it obviously hits home a little bit closer than it does for other nationalities just purely because, you know, country drivers stick together.

'I started the race and I'd gone past the incident several times under the safety car, and I knew it wasn't good. [Wolfgang] Ullrich told me when I got out and Tom had just got in, and I asked if Tom knew. Ullrich said, "No – I'll tell him after he's done his first stint", which was clever strategy by Dr Ullrich.

'But for Tom to be able to resiliently put that into perspective, to the back of his mind, and then with Loïc [Duval] and me come through and win Le Mans in 2013 showed his strength of character. To dedicate it to Allan, that was quite touching. Now that's not to do with the racing driver; that's to do with the human.

'Loïc, for sure, was the energy in our car. He was the real spark of energy you need to rejuvenate, every now and then. And Loïc was our rejuvenation, but it's got to be Tom because of the human, not the driving talent.'

Did you find any drivers difficult to work with?

'Yes – everybody that was fast! We have got to put it in context. You're in a very, very competitive environment. There can only be one winner. So that means if you had a team of two cars, someone has to lose if someone wins. We are all very aware that the light shines on you when you win and it's bloody tough to go home when you don't. I think that brings out different personalities. I don't think you ever have teammates that are not in the same car, who are true friends at the time. [They] can be later, but at the time I don't think they can be true friends. Because, ultimately, if you are at that point where it's into the last corner on the last lap, and one's gonna win the Championship, one's not – it's when all the gloves are off, it's just full-on street-fighting.

'In some teams, the two cars [were pitted] against each other, as opposed to competing against everybody else. I think that can be good, but it can be very disruptive if it's not managed correctly. And invariably, it needs a very strong character to manage these situations.

'But the driver that I probably had the most friction with and has become one of the people that I most respect and trust for guidance was Emanuele Pirro. He and I were in opposite cars for the majority of our Audi

McNish describes 'Dindo' Capello (on right) as the bond between him and Tom Kristensen – and also as an exceptionally quick driver in his own right. (Motorsport Images)

'We are all very aware that the light shines on you when you win, and it's bloody difficult to go home when you don't.'

careers – just by the way it worked out, not for any other reason. He was with Frank Biela, and Tom was their sort-of third driver at the beginning. I was only always with "Dindo" and there were also two Italians, which added to the dynamic of it.

'But Emanuele and I definitely butted heads on a few occasions: we butted heads on the circuit, we butted heads in the briefing rooms. We butted heads quite a few times – always professional, I have to say, but always fighting our own corners. But no question, I think I probably irritated him quite a lot, and certainly at times he irritated me. It wasn't that we had a bad relationship; we were two very, very competitive people.

'Ultimately, as I said, there can only be one winner. What was very interesting for me, and I learned a lot out of this, was two things. When we won Le Mans in 2008, and it was basically going to be his last year, EP was the first person to come up and congratulate us. He said, "The right car won". And that was one big thing for me.

'When he retired and, if I'm very honest, when I retired, my mindset changed. I saw so many different sides to Emanuele, and I realised that, actually, the reason that we probably didn't get on so well all the time was because we were very similar personalities. We were both fighting like hell to win; we had the drive to do it. And ultimately, we were in an extremely competitive environment. Take both people out of that and you realise that personalities do change with the environment. Now we get on really well.'

Who do you think is the best driver of all time, and why?
'That is so subjective. I didn't know – Jim [Clark]; I wasn't around when he was killed, unfortunately. And so really my "all time" starts with James Hunt, Niki Lauda, Jackie Stewart. From watching, it starts with Ayrton Senna, Alain Prost and Nelson Piquet. From me being involved, I had a little experience of Ayrton because of the McLaren testing, but also Michael and Mika. Today, from just watching, it's clearly Lewis.

'Each one moves the benchmark so high, but I think for the skill set and the aura he's got about him, it's Senna without

question. He had a capability to do things on a consistent basis that others couldn't. But I don't think he would have won as many World Championships as Michael Schumacher if he'd still been alive, because Michael was extremely metronomic. That capability to be right on the edge in so many different areas was, I think, Michael's extreme talent. And also the way he was able to drag people around him within the team to work only for him.

'I think we're seeing Lewis Hamilton coming to the point that he's going to move that benchmark forward again. If you take it on numbers, you have to say Lewis, but if you take it on race starts and wins and things, you see Jim, Jackie and Fangio.'

Who have you had the most fun with?
'I had a lot of fun with Mika [Häkkinen] in the 1980s when we were two 18/19-year-olds, going through Europe with Vauxhall Lotus with Allard Kalff, with Heinz-Harald Frentzen, Marco Werner, Justin Bell and David Brabham. In those days it wasn't so corporate. We were following the majority of the European Grands Prix because Opel Vauxhall was a support race. So, for us, watching the Grand Prix was part of the fun of the event. We got into a lot of fun and a lot of trouble as well.

'Mika Salo was also definitely someone that created entertainment, not necessarily corporate entertainment! There were certainly situations where, for example, rental cars got crashed.'

Why do you all have rental car crashing stories?!
'It's not actually us – it's the fact that the rental cars don't have quite the grip of an R18! I think that's the problem. They just don't have excessive amounts of downforce.'

Who was the bravest?
'That's got to be Mika Häkkinen. And that's not brave-stupid. That's brave. When I say brave – throw it in and have the skill set to sort it out. I'm talking fast corners here. And the first time I saw that was at Donington actually, in 1987, when we were doing the Marlboro test and there were six or eight of us going for the two junior seats. It was at the Old Hairpin. I didn't know anything about left-foot braking. There were three pedals in the car, so I was always struggling to work out which one to press! He just left-foot braked through there, and then it was just his car balance and dancing on it.'

Do you have any favourite stories about fellow drivers that you can tell?
'There's two about "Dindo". There was an email group on our system for when we were doing a thing called a shakedown. A shakedown consisted of just driving the car for half an hour, making sure everything was OK, then it'd be packed and sent to base. It meant you flying to Germany, spending the day hanging around a cold, bloody windy airfield to do 30 minutes in the car.

'Anyway, I saw the email coming in and generally not many people wanted to do it. I saw the email coming in and I was actually genuinely busy because I was going to the States. I sent an email back to Steffi, who was in coordination, saying, "Sorry Steffi, I'm in America and so can't do it this time." Within about 30 seconds, "Dindo" sent one back, and this is to the whole group, saying, "Hi Steffi. Sorry, I can't make it either. Because Allan's in America, I'm with his wife in Monaco!"

'I can't remember the year but something called "hats off" was introduced. It was a bladder bag that sat inside the top of the helmet and it had a small pipe that came out the side. In the case of an incident where your neck was injured, they could put a neck support on and they could inflate the bag, which then raised the helmet off your head. They actually have it for motorcycles. I thought it was a really good thing, but we had to put it in ourselves. Because of legalities, the helmet manufacturer couldn't do it.

'We were leading the race and "Dindo" came on the radio and said, "I can't see, I can't see, I can't see." Then he said, "Oh, I can see again." And then a little bit later, "I can't see, I can't see. Oh, I can see again."

'He had to come in for a pit stop because suddenly he couldn't see any longer. We were completely and utterly confused. What the hell was going on here? How can you see, not see, see, not see? As it turned out, the "hats off" system had become dislodged from the helmet. When he braked, the helmet came down over his eyes and pushed the balaclava over his eyes. And then when he accelerated, the whole thing went back again so he could see. He couldn't see in the braking area but could see on acceleration! This was just perfect "Dindo" – he still led the race, could still pull into the pits, but was coming on the radio: "I can't see, I can't see. Oh, I can see again."

'I've been very lucky. I had a 32-year driving career, starting with karting, at a good level and with some great people and teammates. I've met Indy 500 winners, Formula One World Champions, Monaco Grand Prix winners, Le Mans winners – all of these different sort of characters. I suppose there are common threads. For me, every single one has a massive passion for the sport, insane talent, but extreme single-mindedness to get them to that level and to be consistently at that level. But the character you see on television, and the character you see outside of TV, is a very, very different beast. And in that respect, I think you can only find out what people are like when you get them away from their business environment – get someone in the office and get them outside the office, and it can be two different people.

'There's been some teammates that I would like to have driven with. I'd like to have driven more with David Brabham – I only did one race with "Brabs", actually, in a sports car. He was a real thinking driver. He was looking at how to maximise it.

'When you're driving, you focus very much on yourself. You do see what other drivers are doing to maximise their performance, but now I'm able to step back and see it in more detail and then you see a wider view. I developed by trial and error, by trying to think one step ahead.

'[Today] we're on minute detail gains, and it's about a lot more effort and energy and investment by everybody to maximise those tiny details. That creates a situation where I think the requirement to be a top-line professional racing driver is so much 365 days, 24 hours a day now, in comparison to when we were starting out, when you could do it without necessarily putting that total level of effort in.'

Portrait of the artists as young men. McNish (left) with Heinz-Harald Frentzen (centre) and Mika Häkkinen in 1988. (Motorsport Images)

DAVID COULTHARD

Interviewed by **BEN EDWARDS**

DAVID COULTHARD (GB)
Born 27 March 1971

Scotsman Coulthard was immediately successful when switching from karts to cars, and in his first season he won 22 times in 28 Formula Ford starts. That caught the eye of Jackie and Paul Stewart, and Coulthard joined Paul Stewart Racing for Formula Vauxhall Lotus, Formula Three and Formula 3000. By 1993, he was a test driver for the Williams Grand Prix team and was promoted to an occasional race seat in 1994. He got the job full-time in 1995 and won for the first time in Portugal, before moving to McLaren for 1996. There he won 12 more times and was runner-up in the 2001 World Championship. Coulthard retired in 2008 following four seasons at Red Bull Racing.

Which teammates did you enjoy working with the most?
'I wouldn't say I had a really bad relationship with any of my teammates, but I had uncomfortable situations with Damon [Hill]. Ironically, now, [although] we're not best buddies by any stretch because of the generational gap, I have a lot of respect for Damon. We've spent some very nice social times together, since no longer being teammates, but now when I look back on it — we'd lost Ayrton, and Damon must have been under immense pressure. I was under no pressure whatsoever. So I would just come in and say it as I saw it.

'The "highlight" of that particular relationship was at Spa [in 1994] when Rubens [Barrichello] qualified on pole and it started to rain. I think Damon was third and I was on the fourth row. I mentioned [in team meetings], more than once, that Rubens wasn't a good starter. In the morning briefing, I just mentioned it again: "Just be careful of Rubens — he might be a bit bad getting off the line."

'And in front of everyone, Damon said, "If you say that one more time, I'm gonna punch you in the f*****g face," which was quite uncharacteristically aggressive for Damon. He definitely comes from that "stiff upper lip" era and you would expect something a bit more elegant.

'Anyway, I responded with, "OK, let's go outside". I guess that was my instinctive reaction. I was always taught that people who are really going to punch you aren't going to warn you they are going to punch you. They just punch you. So, I kind of figured that if he's threatening to punch me, there's a good chance he doesn't really mean it.

'Anyway, we were obviously talked down by Patrick [Head] or whoever, and then it just went away. So that was a high point, low point in my relationship with Damon.

'Mika [Häkkinen] and I never really had big, big disagreements but sometimes he wouldn't talk to me on the podium. That happened at two events [in 1999] — in Austria when I spun him out at turn two, and at Spa, where we touched at the first corner and I went on to win. He just wouldn't acknowledge me or speak to me.

'Kimi [Räikkönen] just didn't say a great deal to his teammates! Mark [Webber] and I were probably the most relaxed together because I was at a different stage of my career. It was quite clear that Mark was the future and I wasn't.

'With every teammate you have a fallout somewhere. In China in '08, the race was going from wet to dry and you're all out of sequence with tyres, Mark came out on fresh tyres and was behind me and I was behind [Heikki] Kovalainen. He was in the last points-scoring position and the team asked me to move, but I was sure that I could get past Kovalainen. As we were both out of the points, I'm thinking, "No, I'm not moving from a non-points-scoring position when I have the chance of a point."

'Eventually I did get past Kovalainen and got a point and Mark didn't. So, it was the right thing to do. But Christian Horner took us both for a chat afterwards, and it all got a bit heated.

'With Gil [de Ferran], my first teammate, we touched wheels at Zolder in the Opel Lotus and he got a puncture. Then we had to drive back to the UK in a car [together] from Belgium. He never spoke to me the whole way back, including when we were on the boat. But he ended up being one of my best mates.

'I had good relationships with all of them, the most distant being Kimi because he's still racing so he's still in that zone. I think that once you share the highs and lows, you do get to know people pretty well.'

Who had the most sheer pace when you look back at those drivers?
'I guess Mika because he was the longest [duration] teammate I had, and probably at the height of my career. By the time I was with Mark, I had lost some pace. Although I think a high point was really digging deep and out-qualifying Kimi, genuinely, at Suzuka

Coulthard gives a lift to long-time McLaren teammate Mika Häkkinen after the Finn had retired on the last lap of the 2001 Spanish GP. (Motorsport Images)

[in 2002]. It took me a long time to master Suzuka but it shows you can overcome [anything] if you have enough desire.'

That must have really upset him on a circuit like that!
'Yeah, especially when you are known not to be a good qualifier. So that was a double whammy – to be out-qualified by a teammate, and he's not even considered any good at qualifying!'

GERHARD BERGER

Interviewed by **PHILIP PORTER**

> **GERHARD BERGER (A)**
> Born 27 August 1959
>
> Tall Austrian Gerhard Berger made his Formula One debut with ATS towards the end of the 1984 season, and took his first Grand Prix victory two years later in Mexico for the Benetton team. Although he had three seasons alongside Ayrton Senna at McLaren, many enthusiasts most closely associate him with Ferrari. Berger spent a total of six years there, and famously led a team one-two at the 1988 Italian Grand Prix in front of a delirious home crowd. It was the only time McLaren were beaten during that season, and it happened only four weeks after the death of Enzo Ferrari himself. By the time Berger retired following the 1997 season, he had won 10 Grands Prix – the most recent coming earlier that year in Germany.

May I start by asking you for your memories of working with Ayrton Senna?
'We had a great relationship. I started to be aware of his name when I was in Formula Ford. Then I went into Formula Three, and that's where we started to meet each other. With the race in Macau [in 1983] it was quite funny because he won the race; I was third. He had quickest lap and was on pole, everything. But for some reason, they gave me the quickest lap. I saw my records in the evening: "That's not me. I didn't do this lap." And then I went to a party and Ayrton came up to me: "You know, that is my quickest lap that you have." [Laughing] I said, "I think you're right!"

'So you could see, already, how hungry he was for each record, for each success. That was when we started to talk to each other. We were the same age, we had the same interests and we had a good relationship from the beginning. Then he moved into Formula One direct from Formula Three. I was still in Formula Three. And I remember the Formula Three race in Monaco [in 1984]. He was there for the first time in Formula One. I met him there and he says, "Well, I'm waiting for you. When are you coming?" I said, "OK, next year."

'So there was always a dialogue. And then when we were in Formula One, we became for a while very big competitors [rivals] – him in the Lotus, me in the Ferrari, fighting in a lot of races for positions and poles. And then I decided [in 1990] to join McLaren as his teammate. Then of course, another era started because we were in the same car. I have to say I completely underestimated his performance level in all kinds of different areas. But we were again good friends, and even through difficult periods, we managed. In general, I couldn't say anything negative about him.

'He was a Brazilian street fighter who was "playing the piano" in all kinds of ways every day. When you went to a team, he had it already deeply under control. When you go out in the car, he had already a better set-up. He had already the better engine. When you go to the press, he had already stated his position. So he was always ahead of the game. That's why he was as successful as he was. The most important thing is you have people with this capability but then he was also super-talented, super-committed.

'I studied him a lot, of course, because when I drove together with him, I saw that my performance was not enough to beat him. So I had to see where is his weakness, where can I beat him, but honestly I didn't find it.'

How do you think he and Alain Prost compared?
'Well, I have to say, after all these years, it was difficult to be a friend of Senna's and Prost's friend. I think at one stage you had to choose the club. It was not that they wanted this but there was such a big competition going on, such big fights going on and so on. And for me, naturally, being the same age and being friends from Formula Three, I joined the Club Ayrton.

'I have to say when I look back and when I meet Alain today he's as nice as Ayrton was. There is a lot of discussion about who is the best ever. My choice is always Senna. But I had lunch once with Bernie and I said, "Who is the best of all for you?" and he said, "Alain Prost". He was never loved by teams like Ayrton was; he always had to fight. He finished second a lot of times in the Championship. He always got the car right, he always delivered. I still think that Ayrton was the best but Prost was an outstanding driver, with such good feel. I have to say, over all the years, he was an outstandingly nice person too. So both are special people in our sport. And both are, as I say, nice personalities.'

How about Nigel Mansell?
'I always got along with everyone, you know. I can hardly remember – maybe a couple of guys – I didn't like or I had some bad times with. Yeah, you sometimes have difficult experiences but at the end of the day, I got along with everyone and with all my teammates.

'Nigel definitely was not an easy one. Nigel was very different; it was not easy with him. He's always been great and nice to me. He was a quick race driver. He was aggressive on the car, spectacular at certain moments.

Berger on his way to victory in the 1994 German Grand Prix at Hockenheim. (Motorsport Images)

Berger with Ferrari teammate Nigel Mansell (left) and hitching a ride with his good friend Ayrton Senna during their time at McLaren. (Motorsport Images)

Not the same league as Senna or Prost but also a World Champion who deserved to be a World Champion. My relationship was not as close as the one with Senna but it was a nice relationship as well. Good guy, too.

'I feel I am not giving stories that people would like to hear but it's the truth!'

We only want the truth! How about Nelson Piquet?

'Nelson, I rate him very highly as a driver. He had such a smooth style, a quick, smooth style. He was extremely friendly to me but he could be nasty like hell. When I remember the fights between Nigel and Nelson, it was funny for us but, at the end of the day, it was very tough for them, especially for Nigel.

'I liked Nelson's driving style. He was so smooth and fast, and a quality guy too. He was another, as I say with Ayrton, a Brazilian street fighter. The Brazilians always had some speciality. They are always charming, good looking, funny, but when it came to business they had extremely high killer instinct.'

Somebody I have been told is very underrated: Thierry Boutsen?

'Well, I don't think any of this list is underrated because everybody had his chance of success. But Thierry was a completely different person to all of them because he was very closed, very polite, very nice. He wasn't selling himself in a way, maybe, that some other people would do.'

Was he too nice?

'Maybe, yes! Let's say when it comes to the killer instinct, Thierry had the killer instinct just in the car. You don't get into Formula One and win races if you don't have the killer instinct. Piquet, Senna, Prost all had the killer instinct in all areas. It was political. Senna just did his homework every day in a way that meant there was never a door open for anything, for any of the others.

'Thierry, once he was in the car, was a very fast driver. But I think at the end of the day, we can call it too nice. We can say maybe not "playing the piano" in all areas. But a great personality.'

How about Keke Rosberg?

'Keke, I like him a lot. I still have good contact with him, and he's the most straight of everyone. I mean, he just couldn't tell you something different from the truth. In a very Finnish way, he makes a point but with a very good sense of humour.

'And in the car I liked his driving style because he was spectacular, you know, on the street circuit or whatever. And he was a guy of style. I liked it. You know, I liked his rough style. Great car control. No bulls**t. So one of my favourites, I have to say.'

Jean Alesi perhaps never had the success that maybe he deserved?

'Speed-wise, I would say he is the most underrated guy because the speed he had and the car control was quite outstanding. But the package he had was, in certain areas, a long way away from Ayrton or Prost. He had passion; he was very emotional. But the most lovely person of all. He has such a big heart. He was a great race driver, and you could trust him. He was funny. On his day, you couldn't beat him. He was the one who would deserve many more wins than he has on the table.

'He was super, super, super funny. His sense of humour is outstanding and this, combined with his nervous system and his emotions, combined with his speed, it was just fun every day.'

What are your thoughts about Michael Schumacher?

'He's the most interesting character. Because of the tragedy he is in, I would like to say just nice things about him. Because such success combined with such a drama is just something which it hurts me even to think about, and so I'm very happy to see his son now in Formula One because that's what he [Michael] would wish. I will always help wherever I can help because it's great.

'When I remember back, he was a person who, when you met him on holiday or at a party, [was] very nice. I like him. Very German, OK, but very nice! But when he was on the racetrack you didn't trust him because he was capable of doing anything for his success. So you will say, "What do you mean because every one of you guys was doing everything for your success?" You're right, but Senna was wishing [to take] everything to the limit and over the limit, but he would never leave the road of being sporting.

'So when you see Schumacher fighting with Villeneuve, for example, when he

ran into his car, or the same with Damon, or at Monaco for pole position – I think Senna would never have done that. You can say, "Well he did it to Alain Prost in the first corner in Japan." Right, but that was a different story: there was payback from the season before. But Michael was capable of doing it. That was part of his success.

'He is seven times World Champion and the most successful driver until today. I never got that close with him and maybe I would like to have done because when I was out with him and I met him on holiday, when I met the family, they were all super people, but then there were these things that made me a little wary.'

What about Mika Häkkinen?
'I know less of Mika than the others. Mika, in my time, was still young and fighting to make his way. He was super-successful just after I stopped. I think it has something to do with the culture of Finland because, like Rosberg as I already told you, [Mika] was also always straight to the point, no bulls**t. "That's what it is." I always liked him, a cool guy, a good guy.'

Was there anyone you would avoid going wheel-to-wheel with, anyone who you didn't trust?
'I do not think it's about trusting but I wouldn't go wheel-to-wheel with Rosberg. Rosberg was very tough. This was also something [that came] out of Finland. He could cope with everything but you could be sure that he would double the gift back. He was the one you don't play around with too much. It depends whether you mean just with jokes or in the race car. I have to say all the names [we have discussed] actually you could go wheel-to-wheel with because every one was such a good driver.

I wasn't thinking just of the ones we have talked about but anybody you raced against in Formula One?
'It was much more difficult with guys who were not experienced, who were not top level. Sometimes you would prefer to stay away but with these guys [discussed] you like to go wheel-to-wheel with them. I remember with Nigel Mansell at Imola once [and] we had a big, big moment in Mexico: we touched wheels five or six times and he finally overtook me on the outside of the quick corner before the start/finish line but we banged wheels, I think, every lap a couple of times.

'The same happened at Imola on the big, long straight after Tamburello. We were doing more than 300kph, and I banged his wheel and he went on to the grass, and started to spin next to me, and I thought, "Oh s**t, he's dead" because of the speed we were doing. And a couple of laps later, he was on my gearbox again! [laughing] With these guys, we all trusted each other and it was OK.'

I think you have already answered my question as to who, for you, was the best of all time...
'It's always difficult. I think you only can judge who was the best in the era in which you were driving. You have a Jim Clark before [my era]. So I'm saying Ayrton Senna was the best of all time, yes, that's what I'm saying, but can I really compare him with Jim Clark? Can I really compare him with Stirling Moss?

'I look at much more than the statistics. I look at how the person was, how he sold himself, how he brings the success onto the table and so on. And clearly Ayrton is the best – until today. Statistically we have to say Hamilton is outstanding. For me, he is the first guy I see on a level with Ayrton, driving-wise, on the sporting side, but the package of Ayrton, the charm of Ayrton, the fairness of Ayrton on the limit, I think still makes him my favourite.'

Did any of the drivers play tricks on you?
'There is always give and take [laughing]. So, yes, of course.'

Murray Walker told me about some of the tricks you played on Ayrton Senna. Can you recall a couple?
'There's so many but we had such a hard time driving [as well]. I remember once we were fighting each other in qualifying at Imola. I remember once he got out of the car and came over to my car – and I had just done quickest lap after he did quickest lap,

then I did quickest lap, then he did quickest lap. And then we had the last set of tyres to go out again. He took off his seatbelts, got out of the car and came over to me and said, "You know, it's getting dangerous."

'So we really forced ourselves to absolute limits. And then when I'm talking about all the other stuff, it feels like we just have fun and tricks. The reality was, yeah, we did it sometimes but this period was still dangerous, and we were on the limit.'

I understand there was, of course, a very serious side to your racing but there was a more relaxed element to your relationship as well.
'We were staying in Villa d'Este and we used to go by helicopter from the racetrack to the hotel and back. It was contract time and Ayrton and I always discussed the contracts – we were very open with each other and he'd say to me, "OK, today I have this offer… Tomorrow I will do this," and so on. He was involved in the negotiations with Ron Dennis and I was getting a little bit tired [of this] because every day it was the same story. One day, in the morning, he came out and was on the way to the helicopter with his briefcase in his hand. He showed me the briefcase: everything had been done the night before – he'd signed the contract for the next season.

'So we get into the helicopter. He put the headphones on because he was flying the helicopter. I was sitting in the back with all the briefcases – my one, his one – under my legs. Lisa Dennis was sitting next to me. I was a bit bored; I watched from the window. We were approaching the racetrack and then crossing the racetrack and I saw his briefcase just under my legs. So I just started to open the door slowly and I dropped the briefcase out with the contract in, and I closed the door again. Lisa was laughing so much as I watched the briefcase fly down.

'Then we landed and after one or two minutes he came round to my side of the helicopter and looked for his briefcase. He said, "Where's my briefcase?" At the same time, people were screaming because they saw something flying down from the helicopter into the forest and so they came running over the fields where we landed with the briefcase in their hands.

'So he looked at the people running with the briefcase and looked at the helicopter. He said to me, "You didn't throw it out?" I said, "Yes, I did! Here's your briefcase." [Laughing heartily]

'He had a special briefcase from a company that advertised them with an elephant standing on one because they had a special shell [construction] which was composite or whatever. So the briefcase looked quite good after its flight down from the helicopter but inside everything had "exploded" so all the contents were a mess!'

Wonderful. And what about the frogs?
'The frogs was another quite funny one. We were in Australia and I went running in the evening on a golf course and suddenly I saw a fountain and I saw all these huge toads. When I got back [to the hotel], I gave the concierge $100 and I said, "Bring me some of these animals."

'The guy was so happy about the $100 that he made a big pack full of all these frogs. He came back one hour later with, I don't know, maybe 50 of them. Lisa Dennis, Ron's wife, was always very funny and she was always involved in the organising. So I went to reception and picked up [Senna's] room key and we went to his room.

'Then we just opened everything. And we put one of these frogs everywhere. For example, his washbag – open, put the frog in and close again. We put them in clothes bags. We put them in the bed under the sheets so you could see them rocking around. After we put 50 frogs everywhere, we went back to our dinner.

'Next morning he came looking for the idiot [who had done this]. He said, "I had to spend the whole night putting everything out, every single piece out to get all these frogs out of my room." It took until five o'clock in the morning.

'And I said to him, "Where did you find the snake?" Then he was finished. There was no snake. I invented the snake. But then he went to reception to change rooms because he was afraid the snake was still hiding somewhere [laughing almost uncontrollably]!"

Berger's final race with McLaren was the 1992 Australian GP, and he won it. For 1993, he went back to Ferrari – and the first of five years with Jean Alesi. (Motorsport Images)

JACKIE OLIVER

Interviewed by **PHILIP PORTER**

JACKIE OLIVER (GB)
Born 14 August 1942

A versatile and talented driver, Jackie Oliver competed in 50 Grands Prix for Lotus, BRM, McLaren and Shadow, but scored his most high-profile results in sports cars. In 1969, he won the Le Mans 24 Hours and Sebring 12 Hours with Jacky Ickx in a Ford GT40, and two years later added the Daytona 24 Hours and Monza 1,000km in a Porsche 917 with Pedro Rodríguez. He also won the 1974 Can-Am series for Shadow, and later set up the Arrows Formula One team, which over the years ran drivers such as Riccardo Patrese, Gerhard Berger, Derek Warwick, Michele Alboreto and Damon Hill.

How did you rate your various teammates over the years?

'I think the first thing is my experience of driving with a lot of drivers. For me, the skill of the driver and his previous experience are an important element. Some possess greater skill than others but what separates them all is how they apply that skill. Some do it with determination, some do it with flair.'

Who do you think, in your eyes, was the best of all time?

'That is a question of whether or not the skill set that they brought to the profession was appropriate for the time in which they raced. Jimmy Clark clearly had a lot of natural skill, which he applied perfectly by working with Colin Chapman to produce the best cars. Nigel Mansell drove for Lotus, but he drove cars that were different from the type of cars Jimmy Clark had. Jimmy drove little, small-waisted cars with small engines. And so his style of sitting way back in the cockpit, operating the pedals and the steering wheel at such a distance required a lot of finesse.

'Mansell drove cars where you sat well forward in the car because of the downforce requirements and so the driver required a lot of upper-body strength. And so their styles were very different. It's difficult to compare drivers in different periods.'

In your first season in Formula Two, with Lotus, you had Graham Hill and Jim Clark as your teammates. It's always been said, as you just have, that Jim Clark had the natural ability, and Graham Hill had to work hard at it to match him. Would you agree with that?

'Absolutely. I saw it unfold in that way, but didn't recognise it. What Graham achieved was through determination and hard work. Jimmy found that a lot easier, I suspect, but I don't know that. I didn't really know Jim on an individual level. I didn't actually drive with him very much. I just did a few Formula Two races in the same team.'

Of course, Jochen Rindt was absolutely supreme in Formula Two. Why do you think that was?

'Aggression. Jochen was not a nice person. He was very successful at what he did, because of the way he went about it. At a Hockenheim Formula Two race, for example, I finished second because he got me on the last lap because he slipstreamed me. And he said to me, "The best thing about your team, Oliver, is your girlfriend."

'Jochen achieved his success not by natural ability but by getting on top of everybody to make sure he was the winner and it worked. That is a star.'

So when Jimmy was sadly killed, and Graham became leader of the team, you replaced Jimmy at Lotus. How did you find Hill as a teammate? Was he generous and supportive, or not?

'He was very generous – very, very friendly. The only time that I went strongly was at the British Grand Prix. It was a circuit that I had a lot of confidence at. And consequently, I was a lot quicker than Graham. All Graham said to me after the race, when I had led him and kept him behind me, his only comment was, "That was a bit embarrassing for me, wasn't it?" That is the way Graham dealt with the fact that for one moment his teammate was quicker than him.

'The reason why my confidence generally wasn't high is that Colin Chapman had not only lost his best driver, but also had lost his best friend. As a young 20-something, I was a poor replacement. So Colin was having a struggle dealing with the loss of Jimmy and there was no-one else he could put in the cockpit. So it was a difficult period for me; it was a baptism of fire.

'I'll give you an example: the first race I did for Colin, the only advice I got from him, in the cockpit at Monte Carlo, a circuit I'd never been to before, was when he stuck his head in there and said, "Lad, in the whole history of this place, only six people have finished." Which was his way of telling me, "Take it easy. Look after the car. Doesn't matter about the performance. And you'll get a World Championship point if the car finishes." But he used to deliver his advice in that manner.

'So Graham was a good teammate. We did

OLIVER

all the Formula Two races together in '67 and all the Formula One races together in '68. It was the best car in Formula One but, unfortunately, it was not that reliable. And I probably wasn't good enough. But Graham won the Championship and the only race that I finished in was Mexico when I was third, and fifth at Spa [in spite of retiring with two laps to go]. Graham, being the kind individual he was, was quite a good teammate. He treated me as a teammate.'

Defining race: Oliver and Jacky Ickx won the 1969 Le Mans 24 Hours in the very same GT40 that had won there the previous year. (Motorsport Images)

And then of course you went to BRM and had John Surtees as your teammate. He's always had the reputation of being a quick driver but quite difficult.

'Completely the reverse to Graham. But John subsequently taught me a lot of lessons, and I saw his ability and work to succeed. He was a very quick driver. But I saw something in John that manifested itself later in life. His tack at BRM was based on: the car wasn't good enough and, as the lead driver of that team, "I will make the team better so we both succeed." I saw that in him and that ability, unfortunately, was delivered in a rather coarse way. What I mean by that is that everybody in the team, the team owner, the team manager, the chief mechanics, and the driver in the second car, had to be brought into line to do it properly, to make sure we're successful. He went about saying, "The design of the car is crap. And we will change that." So halfway through the season, he brought in Tony Southgate. That ruffled the feathers of the team manager, Louis Stanley.

'John saw the problem of BRM and the way the car was designed, the way the car was developed, and [that] the engine and the people within the organisation weren't good enough and he wanted to change it. I saw that as an asset that John delivered to his job as the senior driver. But that means everybody wasn't doing their job properly. And any distractions away from that needed to be dealt with, but he didn't do it in a nice way. He did it in a very brash way and changed the designer. Now, when you do that in an organisation that you don't own but drive for, if you don't do it nicely, you get resented. So I suffered a little bit from that. John was quite right in what we did, but it

45

Looking down on the BRM at Monaco in 1969. Oliver drove with John Surtees that year, then Pedro Rodríguez in 1970. *(Motorsport Images)*

was the way he went about it.

'He rubbed Stanley up the wrong way. Stanley didn't like him, and Stanley didn't want a driver he didn't like. In me, he had a driver he liked. He thought I was a future star, a British driver for BRM. So there was a conflict. And the team manager, a lovely guy, Tony Rudd – he couldn't stand up to John. And although he would probably agree with Stanley, Stanley was not the appropriate person to run a successful Formula One team – he was driven by other things that John didn't think were important. It came down to John looking at the whole element of BRM needing to be changed, and he brought in Tony Southgate. But in doing so and the way he went about it, he pushed me to the sidelines.

'I remember that one of the first comments when we were somewhere, and there were three cars: mine, the team car and his. I said, "I want that chassis, that engine and that gearbox." So he would say his teammate, Jackie Oliver, was an up-and-coming driver that needed to be suppressed. The team couldn't afford to give the second driver anything that was of use, because it would detract from his car and his success and the team's success. And in some ways he was right. But of course he fell out with everybody in the team. So I stayed with BRM and we got Pedro [Rodríguez].

And then also in that year, 1969, you were in the Gulf-JW Automotive GT40 with Jacky Ickx. What are your memories of driving with him?
'Well, he was another dominant driver. Fact of the matter is, looking back on it, Jacky was better than me in a number of aspects. In the JW Ford GT40, he was number one driver, so he would always want to start the race and finish the race. And in some cases, I think the team looked upon that as being the right order.

'John Horsman spent more time with me than he did with Jacky. When we won Sebring, for example, he came to me and he said, "You seem to be better at night than

Jacky Ickx. We won the race because of your performance at night." David Yorke was probably one of the best team managers that I've seen, because he dealt with all the peculiarities and the dominance of most drivers in a much better way than I've seen anybody do it, and got the best out of them because of the way in which he did it.

'John Horsman and the team manager worked very well together, and the owner of the team organised it in the most effective manner I have ever seen. The reasons why JW was so successful with GT40s and Porsches was because of the management by the team. It was very well run, even to the detriment of Porsche, who saw them as the English succeeding with their car in a much better way than they could run their own team. So, of my two teammates at JW, Ickx was dominant. And Pedro was probably the best teammate I ever had, both in BRM and with JW Automotive.

'Pedro knew that you can win a race with a driver who was as quick as him. At a classic car meeting at Spa 30 years after I drove with Pedro, I met a Spanish-speaking journalist, who said to me, "You know the reason why you drove for Porsche in '71?" I said, "Well, I drove for them in '69. I didn't want to drive for them in '70 because I was busy with Can-Am, and then they came back to me and asked me to drive for them in '71."

'He said, "The reason was that Pedro wasn't very happy with the teammate he had in 1970, and he asked David Yorke if he could get you to drive with him." I looked at the Spaniard and I thought, "Yeah, I believe you actually" – because of the way that Pedro was with me in the team. So with BRM and Porsche, Pedro was the nicest driver I ever drove with. Also, at some circuits, the quickest – Spa being one. I was quicker than him at Brands Hatch, he was much quicker than me at Spa.'

Denny Hulme always seemed like a quiet, laid-back sort of character. Would that be right?

'I got to know Denny more in Can-Am. I drove for McLaren just after Bruce died. It was a bit like Lotus in Formula One when Jimmy died but the difference between the two was that Bruce was not only a driver but the team owner as well. So the loss of Bruce took the heart out of the team. It was a difficult time for the team and probably the worst car they ever produced.

'Denny, as his teammate and his friend was, I suspect, greatly affected by the loss. They had been a twosome in that organisation. A bit like Colin Chapman – he was all things to all people, both in the cockpit and out of the cockpit. I don't think Denny played much part in that.

'If I have to look at Denny's ability, it was OK. His success is certainly attributed to some skill and input but you couldn't really say why Denny was so successful. The car was dreadful that year – I didn't do all the races – but Teddy [Mayer] wasn't a good replacement for Bruce. He wasn't a people person. It seemed to me that Teddy wanted to be the technical manager as well as the team manager. Looking back on it, I think that was a poor combination.

'From 1978 until 2000, I must have hired 15-20 drivers to drive a Formula One car. It was an interesting exercise. Alan Jones, Gerhard Berger – the list goes on, but they were the best ones. You could see the best ones, who went on to greater things. Derek Warwick was very good. He was a bit like Graham [Hill] – not as amusing as Graham, but very similar determination.

'Damon also drove for me. His success as World Champion was driven by the same elements his father possessed. If you read Damon's book, the loss of his father had a bigger effect on him than I realised, than I was aware of at the time when he was driving for Arrows after winning the World Championship. He was angry with his father for not being around for him and that motivated him to succeed like his father had.'

Shooting the breeze at the 1969 South African GP. From left: Hulme, Rindt, Andretti, Beltoise, Oliver and Ickx. (Motorsport Images)

JAMIE CHADWICK

Interviewed by **SIMON TAYLOR**

JAMIE CHADWICK (GB)
Born 20 May 1998

Although Chadwick was also a promising young hockey player, from the age of 15 she decided to focus on motor racing and spent 2013 and '14 racing in the Ginetta Junior Championship. Alongside co-driver Ross Gunn, she then won the GT4 title in the 2015 British GT Championship, and in 2017 she moved into single-seaters. The following year, Chadwick became the first woman to win a race in the British Formula Three Championship, and in 2019 she joined the Williams Driver Academy. She's won the W Series title in both years that it's so far been held (2019 and 2021), and also competes for Veloce Racing in Extreme E.

At the age of 17, you won the British GT4 Championship. Were you aware of the sports car heroes at that stage or were you already focused on Formula One?
'At that point, I wasn't focused on Formula One from a career point of view. As a fan of the sport, obviously I followed Formula One, but at that age I was learning so much about sports cars. I'd had great mentorship and guidance through the guy who coached me at the time, Jonny Adam, and he was someone I looked up to as an advisor, [seeing] the way he pursued his career with Aston Martin and I was inspired by that. I wanted to maybe emulate something similar to what he had done.

'I was, and still am, a massive fan of Le Mans. Tom Kristensen is someone I've always looked up to, alongside Derek Bell, another Patron of Hope for Tomorrow, and a lot of names that I've been fortunate to rub shoulders with early on in my career to get that kind of interest and level of excitement around pursuing a career in sports cars.'

We've got to talk about Extreme E, which is so different to anything we've seen before…
'It's hard to put into words. I didn't expect my career to take me in that direction but I'm enjoying the challenge of trying to adapt to a whole new format of racing that's completely different to anything I've ever done. Being in off-road SUVs in comparison to on-track in single-seaters, it couldn't be further from what I've learnt previously, but it's something I'm very proud to be involved with – raising awareness of climate change and gender equality.

'From a racing point of view, it's an opportunity to compete at a high level against some of my heroes from when I was growing up. To say I'm racing against Jenson Button, Sébastien Loeb, Carlos Sainz – it's something I never thought I'd be able to say.

'Nico [Rosberg] was also at the first race and to spend time with him… again, if I look back to five years ago, I never thought I'd be mixing in paddocks with him. It's really cool to see someone like Nico, with his experience, and now putting that into practice as a team owner – it's good to see what he brings to the team.'

Who is the hero that you ultimately want to emulate? What's your goal?
'The ultimate goal is still to race at the top level of motorsport and, in my eyes, that does remain Formula One. My ultimate hero is an obvious one, but it's Lewis Hamilton. I think what he's achieved, and every weekend you watch his performance, and every weekend that reinforces to me why he is someone I look up to so highly. I don't think I could actually emulate what he's doing at the moment but, at the same time, I'm definitely inspired by him.'

What is it about Lewis Hamilton that you particularly admire?
'I think first and foremost the reason I'm inspired by him is because of his abilities and his talent on the track, but I think that does come from a place from within, and he's a very different character to what we see quite often in sport. But I do think he's authentic. I do think he's true to himself. And that's just the way he is. I think that's something we should push all characters, all drivers, to be like because I don't think I could emulate Lewis by trying to be like him. I would be a rubbish version of Lewis Hamilton if I tried to have the same personality as him, but I really do genuinely think he is authentic, and the life he lives is the way that he is personally. As a result, he drives the way he does. And I think there's a lot to be said for that.'

Chadwick won at the A1-Ring in 2021 on the way to claiming her second W Series title. (Motorsport Images)

ALAN JONES

Interviewed by **PETER WINDSOR**

ALAN JONES (AUS)
Born 2 November 1946

Alan Jones was the son of successful Australian racing driver Stan, and graduated through Formula Three, Formula Atlantic and Formula 5000 before making his Formula One debut in 1975 with Harry Stiller Racing. Later that season he joined Graham Hill's Embassy Racing outfit, then moved to Surtees and Shadow, winning his first Grand Prix for the latter in Austria in 1977. But it was with Williams that Jones hit his stride, winning 11 more times and claiming the 1980 World Championship. He retired at the end of 1981, only to make an unsuccessful comeback with Carl Haas' team in 1985–'86.

Jones shone in Patrick Head's superb ground-effects Williams FW07, which was introduced during the 1979 season. He retired here in Monaco, but his time would come. (Motorsport Images)

'WE FORMED REALLY strong bonds and friendships during my F3 days in the early 1970s. Like a lot of racing people in those days, I shared an apartment with other drivers – in my case, Alan McCully and Brian McGuire. We were three Aussies racing as AIRO [Australian International Race Organisation], pooling some of our resources but basically living hand-to-mouth out of a flat in West London – a bit like Frank Williams, Piers Courage and Charlie Crichton-Stuart had done before us. Brian and I sold Minivans and Dormobiles to poor, unsuspecting Australian and New Zealand tourists, and with the money we made we'd go racing. We had four or five credit cards and we'd use one to buy a set of tyres and then another card to pay off the first card.

'That was the sort of life it was. We were just young blokes, thinking that it would never end and that we were all bulletproof. We were just getting on with it. A bit different from the F3 drivers today, I think. Our diet was based on the food down at the local cafe – usually chips and eggs with a cup of tea, and then down to the pub for a couple of beers.

'Having said that, we were pretty fit. You had to be. One minute we'd be lifting a Formula Ford Merlyn off the back of the flat-top VW; the next we'd be changing gear ratios in the rain at Snetterton. It's just that we didn't have dietitians and helmet-carriers, and all that sort of nonsense, and I think we were better off for it. Those were the formative years and they were teaching you how to deal with different situations – and a lot of those situations were based on not having any money.

'At that time I always used to think that Roger Williamson was very quick but I can't say that we were close friends or anything like that. But Roger was really good. But when I look back on it now, it's amazing to think of how many of those quick F3 drivers just faded away. Colin Vandervell is a good example. It was probably just too easy for him to go back to the family business when things got a bit tough. He was a great guy, a quick driver, but I remember one time he didn't want to race because it was wet. So, I borrowed his set of wet tyres and won with them. He wasn't a bad bloke like that, but I don't know how much he was prepared to get into heartache in order to win.

'In 1973, when I was racing the DART GRD, thanks mainly to George Robinson of Vegantune, I came up against the French for the first time. I guess that was when I kind of discovered how I wanted to go racing. I didn't really befriend any of them – the French or the English. I'd say, "Hi. How ya goin'?" to a Barrie Maskell or a David Purley but mainly I developed into a bit of a loner.

'All came to a head seven years later at the French GP at Ricard, when both the Ligiers qualified on the front row. Typically French, they were already having Champagne celebrations on the Saturday night. Charlie [Crichton-Stuart] was really wound up about it. I'm sure Frank [Williams] used to get Charlie to pick me up from the hotel so that by the time I got to the circuit I was on the rev limiter. It was the Battle of Waterloo all over again.

'So I just wore them down and wore them down and eventually passed them and won. And when I did that, it was a wonderful feeling for a number of reasons because the race prior to that was the Spanish GP, which I'd won and then lost when Jean-Marie Balestre, President of the FIA, declared that it wouldn't be counting for points. So when I won the French GP I had great delight in walking around with the biggest Union Jack I could find and refusing to go up onto the podium until Balestre had left it. Charlie loved all that, of course – and Frank didn't mind it either, although he didn't show it quite as much.

'I initially drove F1 for Graham Hill and John Surtees. John was weird. I have nothing but respect for what he achieved on two wheels and four, but John was also weird because he'd take the car down to Goodwood and test without any wings. He said this was to test the geometry. I'd say, "But John, when you put the wings on you get another couple of tons of downforce and the characteristics of the car completely change," but he didn't want to know. It was always an ongoing battle but I was the guy with my arse in the car. When he put the contract in front of me to do another year, I just said "No". I let all

By late 1979, Jones and the FW07 were the quickest combination on the grid. In Canada, he narrowly beat Ferrari's Gilles Villeneuve after a titanic battle. (Motorsport Images)

and sundry know that if the only way I could do Formula One was with John then I didn't want to do it.

'I did Formula 5000 in the States for a while and loved it. It was a bit more akin to racing in Australia in terms of burgers and chips and that sort of stuff, but at the same time they were also a bit more attuned to life than the English. You know, if it got cold, they had heating and if it was too hot, they had air-conditioning. I used to love going over to the States and Carl Haas was probably the second-best team owner I ever knew, after Frank Williams.

'Again, though, I was a bit of a loner in terms of being mates with anyone. A lot of the American drivers were over the top, taking their pulse rates before they got in the car and all that crap. As someone said at the time, "The worst thing you can do is give a new Lola to an American driver before the season starts because, by the time they 'improved' it, they were two-and-a-half seconds off the pace". I loved them for it, but they were full of s**t.

'I always admired Jimmy Clark. I always admired Stirling Moss. And I had a great deal of respect and admiration for Chris Amon, who I think even to this day is probably the most underrated driver of all time. The guy was incredibly quick and I find it extraordinary that he never won a World Championship, let alone a bloody Grand Prix.

'Clay Regazzoni, my first teammate at Williams, was a good guy. He wasn't political. He kept things pretty much to himself and he was a nice, easy sort of a bloke. I don't think we ever had a cross word. I never used to go to lunch with him, or socialise with him, but at the circuit I didn't have a problem with him at all.

'And I didn't really have a problem with Carlos Reutemann, either. It's not like we used to growl at each other or have verbal

fights behind the caravan. That just didn't happen. It all got blown out of proportion, mainly because of the bloody press. I always found Carlos to be very polite. He was a polite driver and a polite person, in himself.

'In all honesty, I used to keep everyone at arm's length. I never went out of my way to be mates with any of them. I was very much a loner. I don't know if it was out of fear or giving something away – I don't know what it was. I'd never go down to the swimming pool in South Africa or Brazil or Argentina and lounge around with everyone else. I'd more than likely just stay in my room. I was very self-centered. I was there to do a job and that was it.

'I actually used to hate staying at the same hotel as the guys I had to beat. It even got to the point of taking different flights if I felt there would be too many racing people on the flight I originally wanted. I just didn't want to give anything away – even any of my personality traits. I wasn't racing against them as personalities. I was racing against them as things – as objects. You'd recognise a black Lotus or a red Ferrari, and you'd know who was in it – but you never dwelled on who was in it. It was just an object that had to be passed.

'So I'd just say "Hi" to Gilles Villeneuve – no problems whatever – and of course I respected Mario Andretti a lot. He was a really nice guy. I flew back from a test in Argentina with him one year. He was going to the East Coast and I was going back to the house we had in California. I got on very well with him. Of all the drivers I knew, he is the one with whom I still exchange emails from time to time.

'I was probably fairly callous – probably fairly cold – when it came to accidents that hurt other drivers, and this was possibly helped by the fact that I didn't socialise with them. But I do remember vividly going to test at Ricard after Monaco and being the first out of the pits just after Elio de Angelis had gone past in the Brabham. When I got to the fast ess-bend, I could see bits of debris on the track and then smoke coming from the other side of the Armco. I pulled over and jumped out of the car and then over the Armco. His car was upside-down and on fire and his arm was sticking out the side of the car and he was waving it like buggery. I couldn't do anything, because it was that hot, and there was so much smoke and everything. That really got to me – not to the extent of not racing or anything like that, but that's probably the worst accident I've been a party to because I was first on the scene.

'Patrick Tambay was a nice guy. I used to call him Patrick Tampax all the time – me, the Durex Surtees guy! I don't think Patrick knew what Tampax were at that point, but we had a good laugh about it. I guess that was another of my mechanisms: I used to have nicknames for most of the drivers, probably with a degree of disrespect if I think about it now.

'I don't really have any racing friendships today. To be perfectly honest, I think most of today's drivers are a bit precious. I think they all probably believe their own press to a certain degree. It's nice to see a down-to-earth one occasionally – Kimi, maybe. He seems to be a genuine bloke who doesn't mind a drink and is a bit of a larrikin away from the track, but apart from that I think they're all too analytical, too guarded. They won't say anything in case they upset somebody – and that's just not my way.

'I guess ultimately my dad, Stan, had a big influence on me. He was a very, very quick driver. He used to abuse me if I didn't win and if I did win he'd say, "Well, you should have won." He was a very hard taskmaster. He helped me as much as he could, but

> **'In all honesty, I used to keep everyone at arm's length. I never went out of my way to be mates with any of them – I was very much a loner.'**

towards the end of his life he started having strokes and losing money, and all sorts of other difficult stuff.

'He came over to England to spend the last years of his life living with me. He said he wanted to be buried in a lead-lined coffin so the worms wouldn't get at him, and he wanted to have a telephone in his coffin in case he wasn't dead. He partly got his wish, because he died in England and had to be flown back to Australia, and all coffins had to be lead-lined if they were on an aeroplane. But I don't think we managed a phone...'

MARK BLUNDELL

Interviewed by **MARK COLE**

MARK BLUNDELL (GB)
Born 8 April 1966

Blundell made his name in Formula Ford before moving straight into Formula 3000 for 1987. He then served his Formula One apprenticeship as a Williams test driver and got a race seat with Brabham for 1991. He went on to drive for Ligier, Tyrrell and McLaren, and was also successful in sports cars. In 1990, he put his Nissan on pole position for the Le Mans 24 Hours with one of the most memorable *banzai* laps ever seen at La Sarthe, and he won there two years later for Peugeot. Blundell moved to CART racing in America after leaving Formula One, and in 1997 he won at Portland, Toronto and Fontana.

Of all the drivers you raced against in your career, which ones stood out for you in each decade?
'It may surprise you, but in the 1980s it was Dave Coyne – I raced against him in 1984 and 1985 in Formula Ford 1600 and 2000. He won everything and he was an outstanding talent. But he never made it to the top.

'In the '90s it was Ayrton Senna. He was the very best driver I raced against on track; there was no better driver out there on a Sunday afternoon.'

Which drivers were the best teammates?
'Martin Brundle. We were at Brabham and Ligier together, and he was the complete package, a team "mate" in both meanings of the word. We were and still are very close. But Mika Häkkinen was the driver who put me under the most pressure on track and in the garage when we were at McLaren together in 1995.'

Did you find any drivers difficult to work with?
'Whenever you have professional drivers on the same team, there is always going to be politics both on the track and off it, there are always ups and downs. It's all about understanding those politics, and optimising the environment around them, and 99 per cent of the time that's outside the car. So no names...'

Who do you think was the best of all time and why?
'It was Ayrton Senna; both on and off track, the very best. I base that on coming to know him and understanding him, his choices career-wise. He was the complete racing driver, the whole 360 degrees.'

Who did you have the most fun with?
'Again, Martin Brundle. We were F1 teammates for two years with Brabham and Ligier, and we shared everything – flights, hotels, rental cars, and did everything together. We are still close friends today, almost 30 years later.'

Who was the bravest?
'Me! Or perhaps Nigel Mansell. He was so determined; he had a sturdy undercarriage and he could take the setbacks that others might not.'

Do you have any favourite stories about fellow drivers?
'Yes! Martin Brundle and I having such similar names always caused huge confusion in Japan, where our surnames were spelt the same in Japanese characters – and of course we were both M.

'So when you're presented with your teammate's airline boarding pass and you're sitting in seat 1A, and he's put in 69F, you can imagine there's a huge amount of fun – when he'd paid for a First Class ticket and I hadn't...'

Blundell drove for McLaren alongside Mika Häkkinen in 1995. The Flying Finn was among his most challenging teammates. (Motorsport Images)

BRIAN REDMAN

Interviewed by **PHILIP PORTER**

BRIAN REDMAN (GB)
Born 9 March 1937

Brian Redman is one of the most successful sports car drivers of all time, having won the Spa 1,000km four times, the Nürburgring 1,000km twice, the Daytona 24 Hours twice, and the Targa Florio. During the mid-1970s, he won three consecutive Formula 5000 Championships in America, despite strong opposition from the likes of Mario Andretti, and although he raced in only 12 World Championship Grands Prix, he finished on the podium second time out. Redman continued to race into the 1980s, when he was part of the TWR-Jaguar and Aston Martin sports car teams, and more recently he's been a regular – and popular – supporter of historic racing.

Iconic sight: the Gulf-JWA Porsche 917 of Redman and Jo Siffert (inset, Motorsport Images) completes another lap on its way to winning the 1970 Spa 1,000km. (Corporate Archives Porsche AG)

Who was your best teammate?
'Well, I was extraordinarily lucky in that respect, driving with Jacky Ickx in 1968 in the Gulf Ford GT40, and in 1972 and 1973 in the 312 PB Ferrari. But then also in '69 and '70 with the great Jo Siffert. So really, I had the best co-drivers in the world at that time.'

Did you find any of them difficult to work with?
'No, but I was the number-two driver so I made it my business to be comfortable with whatever they did. Both of them were shorter in height than I was, so the seating position in the car wasn't really perfect for me, but I got used to it.'

Who do you think was the bravest driver?
'Well, probably Siffert, who was flat-out all the time, whatever the race. Jacky was much more sensible, but also extremely smart, even though at that time he was pretty young. When I first drove with him, at the 1967 Kyalami Nine Hours, he refused to do the Le Mans start. So he strolls across the track, jumps in, belts himself in and off he goes. By that time we're about a lap behind. Not only that but very early on he comes into the pits – faulty oil pressure gauge, I think, and so now we're quite a long way behind. But we keep going and of course take the lead and win. John Wyer was kind enough to mention after the race, "And now we've found the perfect co-driver for Ickx."'

Who was the most fun?
'Siffert, I think. He was always ready for a lark of some kind. In particular, I think of Spa-Francorchamps in 1970 with the John Wyer Gulf 917. I'm heading towards La Carriere and I'm running probably at about 180, and I turn in and it goes sideways as my left-rear tyre came off the rim. I'd read in a motor racing book that if you let go of the steering wheel in that circumstance the Ackermann [steering geometry] would straighten it, so I let go and it went straight. I come back into the pits and as I get out, Siffert falls on the floor laughing. I said, "What's the matter with you?"
'He said, "Brian, you are the colour of your overalls", which in those days were white!'

Turning to Formula One, and in particular your McLaren year, can you describe what Denny Hulme was like as a driver?
'Well, I don't like to say too much. Really he was probably the only top-line driver that I never got on with for various reasons.'

How about Jody Scheckter?
'In 1973, in Formula 5000, he was a wild South African. But I think, as may be the case with many Formula One Champions, he was determined to be World Champion. And he crashed all over the place – I mean, it was unbelievable – but not much in the race, always in practice. He was so determined that, when we got side-by-side at the fourth race at Mid-Ohio, he turned in and hit me. So the last race was at Seattle Raceway, and Jody and I are again side-by-side going into a tight corner where there isn't room for two cars. Neither of us lifted, so we hit. Despite this, we never got into any arguments. He's a great guy.'

Did you race against Jackie Stewart very much?
'No, not very much. I didn't know him very well at all. We met at the Formula One races that I did. And he did appear at Sebring one year, trying to get all the Formula One drivers to sign a declaration that they wouldn't race at Spa.'

So we've talked about Siffert and Ickx. You obviously rated them very highly.
'Yes. Let's take 1969, when there were 10 factory drivers in the Porsche team, and Siffert was basically the fastest. I'm sure there are several drivers who wouldn't agree with that. But basically, he was. And that was why, on the Monday morning after the first race of the 1969 season, in Daytona, team manager Rico Steinemann said to me, "Brian, would you go as number-one driver and choose your own co-driver? Or will you go as number two to Siffert?" And I just thought we'd win more races if I went as number two.'

Thinking of a few other chaps, how do you rate John Fitzpatrick?
'Well, terrific. He was a real specialist in the [Porsche] 935s, and other cars. Most drivers finish up in one particular niche where they spend most of their career. I know that Fitz raced Minis but I don't know whether he did much single-seater racing. And again, some drivers choose not to take the single-seater route and become very, very good — best in the business — in whatever they choose.

'We won a couple of races together. We won the Mosport Six Hours in the Dick Barbour 935. And we raced together at Le Mans in 1980 with Dick.

'John was an expert with the 935s. It was very important that you were able to fully control the [turbo] boost without damaging the engine and John was one of the few experts who, like Rolf Stommelen and Bob

Redman in the nimble Porsche 908/03 at the 1970 Nürburgring 1,000km. (Motorsport Images)

Wollek, knew exactly how to fine-tune the boost level.'

How about Jackie Oliver?
'Well, the first time I ever met Jackie was in 1965 at Rufforth, England, I think in an Elan. Yes, he was very good. But he was also a brilliant businessman, which I never was.'

What about Andretti and the Unser brothers, Al and Bobby – quick, very quick or average?
'Mario was the only one of the USAC group who was really quick from the get-go. The others were all quick but they were still figuring it out to some degree. Mario and I raced pretty hard against each other for two years. We never touched wheels, never had a cross word, but then we didn't talk to each other much either.

'At the Pocono race in '75, there was a tight corner behind the pits, a left-hander. Bobby Unser was there and I just shot down the inside. After practice he said, "Hey Redman, what the hell are you doing, passing me on the inside like that?"

'I said, "I left you plenty of room", to which he replied, "Is that the way you road-race guys do it?"

'I nodded and he said, "Okay, now I know." He was a great, great man.'

Pedro Rodríguez could be extremely quick, couldn't he?
'Yes, fantastic really. We were teammates in the 1970 John Wyer Gulf factory Porsches. And I had co-driven with him at Montlhéry in the 1969 Paris 1,000 Kilometres in a Matra. He said to me after the race, "Brian, it is a great pleasure to have a co-driver who is almost as fast as I am." Oh, he was great. Pedro was great, no question.'

What made him so good?
'I think he was pretty thoughtful. He just wasn't flat-out all the time. But he had the ability, like Ickx in many ways, to have tremendous speed when necessary.'

Who was the best driver, do you think, in the wet?

'I know Pedro's drive at Brands Hatch in 1970 was outstanding, but I don't think there's too much to choose between Ickx, Siffert and Rodríguez in the rain. They were all exceptionally good. No question.'

So is there anybody else we should be talking about? Someone you respected or felt was especially good?
'In the very early days, there were some people that you never hear of, people nobody's ever heard of, who were so good in their own way – like Harry Ratcliffe, who drove probably the fastest Morris Minor 1000 in the world. Great, great guy. And Allan Staniforth, who was a *Daily Mirror* journalist. Brilliant. Wrote the book on suspension design and built his own cars. Fantastic people you never really hear of.'

Thinking of Formula Two, Jochen Rindt for a long time seemed to be pretty unbeatable. And even against some of the established top Formula One guys. Why was he so good?
'If you look at any era, there's always somebody who stands out, isn't there? And in many ways, even at the top level, it makes you wonder why we even bother when they are clearly the best.'

Who do you think was the most versatile?
'Vic Elford was brilliant, though not quite as good as he thought he was.'

And the quickest of all?
'Jimmy Clark, and then probably Jochen Rindt.'

Did you ever learn anything from any of the other drivers?
'Well, I did some races with Jim Clark in 1967-'68 in Formula Two, and he introduced me to something that, to this day, I still maintain. That was when physical exercise was just starting to raise its ugly head, so I said, "Jimmy, do you like exercise?"

'"Och Brian, I exercise every day."

'I said, "You do?"

'"Och, I lift my leg to get into bed at night."

'So I've been doing that ever since.'

DEREK WARWICK

Interviewed by **LOUISE GOODMAN**

DEREK WARWICK (GB)
Born 27 August 1954

'Del Boy' had an unusual path to Formula One in that he started his career racing stock cars. He won the 1978 Vandervell British Formula Three Championship, and made his Grand Prix debut three years later for Toleman. He moved to Renault for 1984, and turned down a Williams drive for 1985 just as Frank's team was coming good again. Then, in 1986, Ayrton Senna blocked a potential move to Lotus. Warwick continued in F1, but thereafter his greatest successes came in sports cars. He drove for TWR-Jaguar, but it was with Peugeot in 1992 that he won both the drivers' title and the Le Mans 24 Hours.

Which drivers would you say were your best teammates?
'I enjoyed Patrick Tambay in '84 and '85 – an absolute gentleman, lovely guy, super quick, very professional. I suppose I enjoyed it because you knew that you could trust him. There were a few of my teammates that I wouldn't really trust. He was fun. He taught me how to live, he taught me a few French ways of living. We really did have lots of fun and spent a lot of time down in the south of France. We ate together, we would drink together. We did a lot of testing at Ricard so we spent a lot of time in Bandol and just had lots of fun.

'At the beginning of '85, Renault lost all the good guys to Larrousse and Ligier and places. So they tried to make the team up with some guys from Renault production. And the car was sh**e. We went to Rio testing in January '85 and it was like three seconds off the '84 car. Patrick and I went out on the razz and we met a few of the guys and we got absolutely paralytic, and I remember waking up in the middle of the night on the 35th floor of this apartment block that was in the slum area of Rio somewhere, with Patrick in the same room. I was on the floor and I remember looking up thinking, "Where the f**k am I?"

'I looked at Patrick and we looked at the front door, and it was one of those doors that had like 15 locks on it. I'm thinking, "How are we supposed to even get out of this place?" Basically, we got this door unlocked and we both had these bloody Rolexes on, ran down the stairs because the lifts didn't work – it was that kind of place – and we ended up in the slums of Rio and we just ran and ran and ran and ran until we found a taxi or civilisation and went back to the hotel. It was a bit frightening because in Rio you do not want to be in the wrong place.

'Patrick could also be a naughty boy. I remember on a flight back from somewhere, we were in First Class and he was with a very fit and beautiful young lady. He was divorced or separated from his California wife, I think. After take-off Patrick had this silly smile on his face and then disappeared for maybe half an hour to the toilets with this young lady. That's a club that I've never joined, by the way. It's something I'm still working on!'

Did drivers have more fun in your era, do you think?
'We had much more fun. I mean, honestly, we would be either locked up, divorced, or shot today if we even tried to do half of what we got up to. Louise, it was 10 times more fun. I look at the drivers today and feel it's just different. Are they more committed? I don't believe they are. Do they have more to do in the car? 100 per cent. Are the cars today more difficult to drive? In many, many ways, yes. But ours were, for sure, more dangerous. The cars broke all the time, had 1,250bhp in qualifying – it was just different.

'Today's drivers have to be more careful with what they do and say because of the world we live in; they are generally more serious, so how can they have fun with phones and cameras following their every move? I really don't want to use the word more "professional" because we were professional, or at least I was for that time. I worked bloody hard in the team, I worked hard on my fitness. But I have to say that these guys now arrive by private jet, they get picked up by the team PR people, go to the circuit, do a million interviews, which we didn't, do their track walk, work with their engineers on the computer, and when they're not on the computer, they're in the simulator…

'Social media is so big now, you would just get into trouble if you got up to half of the things that we did back in the '80s and early '90s, that's for sure.

'I think you played hard for two reasons. One is because that was the era you were born in and drove in. But also because there was a lot of danger and tragedy around you – something like 12 or 13 drivers died in the 12 years I was in Formula One, including my little brother. I think you made the most of your life for sure. We worked hard and played hard.'

Who did you fear most as a competitor?
'I didn't fear anyone. I respected a lot of the drivers, especially in the early days, the Niki Laudas, the Reutemanns, Pironis, the

Warwick spent two years with Renault, and enjoyed his time with teammate Patrick Tambay. This is Monaco in 1984. (Motorsport Images)

Arnouxs, the Prosts, because they were great, great drivers. I can even go back to 1982 when we had the drivers' strike. That's when I really got myself established as a fellow driver, because you were with them for 36/48 hours, whatever it was. You were sleeping on a mattress next to Carlos Reutemann or Niki Lauda or Gilles Villeneuve, people like that. But I was never frightened of another driver.

'I think there's certain drivers that you knew were different. Whether it was a sort of mystery that they created, or whether there was a Godlike feeling that they brought in with them, and that's obviously Ayrton Senna. I've been to many drivers' briefings, and Prost and Mansell and those sort of guys walked into the room and you never really looked around. But when Ayrton came into the room, he brought a different feeling to that room. He looked to be walking on water, he really was that different.

'And of course I had that love-hate relationship with him where he screwed me over for the '86 season [Senna blocked Warwick's move to Lotus because he felt the team didn't have the resources to support two "number one" drivers], but he's still my hero. I've got a replica helmet of his in my study.'

Apart from Ayrton, did any other drivers have that mythical quality?
'No. A lot of drivers you respected, like three-times World Champions and just World Champions, but you never had that same feeling as when Ayrton walked into the room.

'Like everybody, we had teammates we didn't really get on with. I've always said that Brian Henton from 1980 Formula Two taught me how to survive in a very cut-throat world called motor racing. He was definitely devious and would hide what he could from me. He was a devious little bugger that you knew was trying to screw you over at every moment. I won't say that I carried that on through my career, but it was a caution that you could take with you to the next team and driver. It's not a secret that your biggest competition was always your teammate, because he's the only person you could really be judged against.'

What qualities did the legends have that made them different?
'I think you see amazing speed with some drivers in unofficial testing that they don't bring to the weekend – whether that's nerves, tension, whatever. A good example of that is someone like Andrea de Cesaris – super lovely guy. During a test, he would be really quick and up there and not crash. You take him to the weekend and, I think with McLaren, he crashed in 15 of 16 races or something ridiculous. So there are people that act differently at race weekends.

'I think we all have the same qualities in terms of commitment, some more than others. Some are fitter. You could see the drivers that didn't train. The difference between a good driver, a great driver and a legend is less than a quarter of a per cent for each one of them. So were Prost and Senna better than the other drivers? I think they were a quarter of a per cent better. But that was the way they led their life. They were also lucky with the cars they ended up in. I think they were obviously smart. Could they be any more committed than people like myself? No. I was totally committed. But when I look back now, was I selfish enough?

'I think that's a better word. It's selfish, the way Ayrton acted over that whole situation of kicking me out of the team, before I even got in the team, for the '86 season. That's the ultimate selfishness. He didn't care a s**t about anything else, except him. He wanted the number one mechanic, the number one engineer, he wanted the spare car, he wanted everything and he would do almost anything in order to create that situation. And that's why, God rest his soul, Johnny Dumfries ended up with my drive. So yeah, I think it's selfishness.

'I've always thought of myself as being the most selfish, unselfish person you will ever meet. I'm totally selfish when I want to do things like Formula One, when I went testing, when I was training, it all came first. I remember when [my wife] Rhonda was having our second child, Kerry. It was the weekend of Monza and she was seriously pissed off that I just packed my bag and left for Monza, when maybe I should have supported my wife! She thought that was selfish – and how I was selfish when I

cradled Gilles Villeneuve after his accident and later died at Zolder. I had pulled him out of the catch fencing and raced the next day. She could never get her head round that sort of stuff.

'So we're all selfish; I think there's a level of selfishness. We're all committed; there's a level of commitment. We're all fit; there's a level of fitness. So there's lots of little modules that make up the super drivers. It's the same whether you're a legend of tennis, golf or business. You know, I think there are quirky people around in this world of all sports and business that are the Ayrton Sennas, are the Alain Prosts, are the Niki Laudas of our world. The unselfish bit was that, when I finished doing everything in preparation for motor racing, I gave my family every bit of time I had left.'

Were there any drivers you knew who had a reputation before they got on track in terms of the way that they would behave on track? How about teammates first?
'Well, you expect a lot from your teammates, otherwise they wouldn't have been brought into the team in the first place. There were teammates that were disappointing: Teo Fabi, for me, was terribly disappointing. Sure, he was quick, but there were certain parts of his character I didn't like. It really hurt me and a lot of drivers when, during the strike of '82, he crawled out through the toilet window and went back to the team during the strike. People like Laffite and Arnoux were so upset they promised that he would never ever pass them in a race ever again. So there were people like that.

'Bruno Giacomelli – his season in '78 in Formula Two is legendary. In the [March] 782 he won the Championship and he was unbelievable. When he came to Toleman, though, he was just disappointing. He was lazy. We would have a debrief and I'd always debrief first, and he would just say, "Same as Derek, same as Derek," and not contribute, not help the team progress as much as we would all like.

'Patrese – lovely, lovely guy and someone you could look up to and you could trust. Patrick Tambay was the only driver I could actually put my hand up and say that I would trust him 100 per cent. I met him in Italy recently and he said, "Thank you, Derek. I understand you said that I was your favorite teammate, and you could trust me." He said, "Question I wanted to ask you." I said, "What's that, Patrick?" He said, "Could I trust you?" I said, "Absolutely f***ing not." He just laughed.

'Eddie Cheever. I was Eddie's teammate for four years, one with Jaguar and three with Arrows. And we definitely had a love-hate relationship. We did fall out a few times, but got on more times.'

What kind of things would you fall out over?
'Eddie used to get really upset by what the guys in the press would say about him. And if I mentioned things the press said, he would really get upset with me.

'During qualifying at Monaco in '89, I put the car on the third row, sixth quickest, and I was out on another qualifying lap, which was way, way up [on time]. And he baulked me – just after the Swimming Pool and before Rascasse. It was deliberate. As I went by, I put my hands up, like you do, and he gave me the middle finger. Well, I just saw red and I put him in the barrier. Remember, this is my teammate. I put him in the barrier. I think he bent his front wheel back or something and couldn't do his lap.

'I got back to the pits and I was talking to Ross Brawn. I said, "Ross, if you look over my right shoulder, you're gonna see a very irate American climbing over the debris fence. If I was you, I would try and slow him down a bit because he and I are going to have a fight!" I can't really remember what happened after that.

'But Eddie was a sulker, too, so he didn't speak to me until Phoenix. We were going to a USF&G promotion and I came down in the lift – I always put him on a lower floor, just to make him feel worse (joking, Eddie). He got in, looked at me, and with only two people in the lift, turned his back on me. We're going down, down, down in this lift, and I said, "Eddie, this is f***ing childish". He turned around and laughed his head off. And that was it. We were back friends again. But it took that time to get it out of Eddie really.

'To be fair to him, when I had cancer, he rang me quite regularly to see how I was and keep me motivated and cheerful. And that's the Eddie I remember, the caring, loving Eddie. Teammates are an interesting mix. You have got to remember that they are your biggest competitor. But he was a good teammate.'

Were there some drivers who you would deliberately try to out-psych before you ever got out on the track. How much a part of the racing driver's mentality was that?
'Everyone. You had to get into the head of your teammate, not always in a bad way because it depended on the driver. When you were teammates with people like Yannick Dalmas, in '92, when we won Le Mans and the World Championship, I could switch him on and off like a switch. It was as simple as that. I could make him two seconds slower or half a second quicker. I

> *'"Ross, if you look over my right shoulder, you're gonna see a very irate American climbing over the debris fence. If I was you, I would try and slow him down a bit because he and I are going to have a fight!"'*

didn't really like the half a second quicker button very much, but he was somebody that was just too vulnerable, too soft. And that's why he never, I think, made it in Formula One. He just was not strong enough mentally and hard enough.

'David Brabham: you didn't have to switch him on and off, you didn't have to get inside his head because he was too genuine. He was a nice guy. He came in as our back-up driver in sports cars and I remember the first race after Paul [Warwick] had died was Nürburgring. And he helped me through that weekend – he was my teammate and we won the race.

'So you respect people like that and there's no way you're going to do anything dirty, or even think about doing anything dirty, to a driver like that. And so there's certain drivers that are just nice people.'

The strain shows during a challenging 1979 season in Formula Two. He joined Toleman for 1980, opening a path to Formula One. (Motorsport Images)

Were there any drivers who would always try to out-psych others or play those mind games?
'Brian Henton. He would do anything to slow you down – mentally, physically. Having said that, there was a driver killed at Hockenheim – I crashed in turn one with Mike Thackwell and my wheel came off and went into the cockpit of Markus Höttinger. I'm unsure if he was killed instantly, but from what I understand he put the throttle down in an unconscious state and crashed about half a mile up the next straight.

'I didn't know about it, and the press attacked me viciously. "What do you think now that you've killed a fellow racing driver?" and used those words. And Brian Henton protected me. So, as much as you hate your teammate, and you want to hurt him mentally, he is also the first person to protect you. It's a really very weird situation. We're very complex, confused people.'

Confused, yes. Complex…! Were there any drivers that you competed against in either F1 or sports cars who you could see trying to play games with people the whole time?
'Schumacher. Schumacher in '91 when he was driving for Sauber Mercedes [in sports cars]. He was a nasty piece of work, he really was, and I think he would use all the mind games that were possible.

'But another thing I remember from that year in particular is you had the three Mercedes young guns, who were [Karl] Wendlinger, [Heinz-Harald] Frentzen and Schumacher – the three greatest drivers at that time from Germany. But, funnily enough, I only remember racing against one of them. And that was Schumacher.

'He was the real deal, even back then in those early days. You always knew that if your stint coincided with Schumacher, you were in for a tough stint. When I came back again at the Nürburgring in '91, after Paul had died, we were quite strong opponents to each other. He went out, took pole. I took pole. He took pole again. I went out to take pole back. I saw him coming and I sort of half got out of the way, a little bit intentionally, like we do as drivers. It stopped his lap and coming out the back of one of the corners, he just drove across me and took off my left-front wheel, as I was about to start my qualifying lap.

'My emotions, Louise, at this time were as high as they can get when you have just lost the biggest hero of your life: my little brother. I came in hopping on three wheels and it was unbalanced with the left-front gone. As I went past the Mercedes pit, I was already trying to get out of the door and the car was still doing maybe 20-30mph. The mechanics, knowing what's going on, were running towards me to stop the car. I jump out, took my helmet off, throw it down, run into the Mercedes pits, and [Jean-Louis] Schlesser was taking off his helmet. I actually thought it was Jean-Louis. So I cock a right hook and was just about to punch him. And he shouts, "No, no, no, Derek. Schumacher." And as I look around, Schumacher was running out through the back door. So I set off after him.

'By now we've got press, cameras, mechanics hanging off me. Went through one of the Mercedes trailers, out through the front, down the side, through another Mercedes trailer. And then as I got to the little debrief room at the front of the second Mercedes truck, he started shutting the door on me. I barged through and there was a massage table. It was obviously a fitness room or something. I had him over the back of this fitness table, trying to hit him, with Jochen Mass, who was his teammate, holding on to me, trying to stop me and pulling me off, with Jean-Louis Schlesser saying, "Hit him, Derek, hit him."

'That got some bad press for Michael, and the ADAC said that Michael could race as long as he came and publicly apologised to me. After morning warm-up, he came down and he never looked me in the eye and said, "I understand your situation, your brother and everything else", which I would have said had it been the other way around. And he just looked at the ground, never looked at me once and just mumbled something that I suppose resembled "sorry". And that was it. That was good enough for the ADAC and he obviously raced.'

Did you ever revise your opinion of him from those early days?
'Of course I have. It would seem that Michael is not the same Michael as when he was racing. It would seem that he's now locked away in his home in Switzerland. I would do anything to see Michael bouncing back into the paddock again. I have never borne grudges – Senna being a good example. In some ways he stopped my career, but I don't blame him.

'Another good thing, and this is worth saying, at Paul's funeral there was the most amazing amount of flowers and wreaths, and it was just unbelievable – from Senna, from Bernie Ecclestone, from the FIA, from everybody. And I just think that is our community drawing together. That is what you've got to remember: as hard as we might be, as difficult, complex people we might be, we support in the hour of need.'

Did you used to sit down and have dinner with other drivers?
'Not really. You do with teammates because of sponsors, etc, and with Patrick many times. I think you always worked so hard in your team and with your teammate that they became your soulmate. They become the person that you would go to. I think you had certain people within your family, or, for me, it was even journalists like [Nigel] Roebuck, [Alan] Henry and [Maurice] Hamilton. They were my three go-to people that I would talk to about different drives and that sort of stuff, not having a manager. Even people like Nigel [Mansell], who obviously I knew quite well – he was somebody that I liked, I admired, I respected, but not necessarily somebody I would have Sunday lunch with.

'Martin Brundle I've got to know really well, and Mark Blundell. We meet up now once or twice a year – what we call the Rat Pack – and I'm friends with them now, Louise, but I wasn't really friends with them then. I didn't really want to be friends. We lost too many of our friends and, although our era was safer than the era before, it was still a dangerous era to be in. There were a lot of drivers that were killed – people like Manfred Winkelhock, Villeneuve, de Angelis… There were too many people injured or killed, so I didn't want to be that close to them, I'll be honest with you. I had enough suffering with Paul and definitely with Villeneuve when he passed. If I look at today's drivers, does

George [Russell] get on with Lando [Norris] and with Lewis [Hamilton] – ie, the three Brits? No. Of course they speak and they say hello but I don't think they go to Sunday lunch together, that's for sure.'

Apart from the 'Rat Pack', who would be the drivers that you would now think you'd love to sit down and have dinner with, be they dead or alive – people who you think would be the most appealing characters?
'It's a great question. A lot of them. I'd like to understand what made people like Rene Arnoux be a bit strange. What would make Prost so focused? What would make Piquet so difficult and always need to be nasty to most of his fellow countrymen? What made Senna have this unbelievable belief in not just himself but life and God, and all that sort of stuff?

'And then there's the other people – you're gonna have fun so who are you gonna invite? You're gonna have Gilles there for sure. Depailler, Laffite – those sort of people. I think they were fun drivers. Patrick [Tambay], for sure. Are you going out to find out more about what made them different from you, why they won more, why Schumacher won 91 Grands Prix? Maybe you could get to know them now, but you wouldn't have been able to get to know them then.

'I think Keke Rosberg, Kimi: I'd love to spend a couple of days with him. I don't think my liver would survive! Mika Salo: what a great guy, one of the funniest. And

Warwick spent three years at Arrows with Eddie Cheever. They're pictured in close company at Monaco in 1988. (Motorsport Images)

when he talks about Kimi, he talks with such fondness, such laughter, such fun. So Kimi would be at the top of my list, I think, of today's current drivers.'

You mentioned the 2021 British drivers. What's your assessment of each of them?
'Well, not much you can say about Lewis, for sure. He's the most complete driver I've seen in all the years I've raced. You put him up there with Schumacher and Senna and Prost and Piquet, all those sort of guys, if not just slightly above. How Lewis brings a better Lewis every year, every race, his experience, his devotion, love for the sport… He's a legend, and they come along every 10 years. It doesn't matter what sport, you're talking about Sampras, or Federer

Warwick was just as quick in sports cars as he was in single-seaters. In 1992, he won Le Mans with Mark Blundell and Yannick Dalmas. (Motorsport Images)

> '*Seb sits down and the Chairman says, "Right, OK guys, we'll just talk about your incident at the end of the race." Kimi just stands up and says, "Guilty".*'

In recent years, Warwick has become a highly experienced, no-nonsense presence in the F1 stewards' room. (Motorsport Images)

or Djokovic, or whatever. They come along very rarely. [Tiger] Woods, he's up there with those kinds of guys.

'The other two Brits? I think they are the two most impressive, amazing drivers that ever came through the BRDC's Young Driver Programme, which was the McLaren *Autosport* BRDC Young Driver of the Year scheme. We've had some great drivers like Oliver Rowland, Dan Ticktum, Jake Dennis... all those sort of guys won that award. But when Lando and George received the award, they were head and shoulders [above the others], they were unbelievable. And I think George was with Albon so he had a really tough year too. But he was just different. And I would say to you now that we have the next 10-15 years of great, great drivers – World Champions, if they find the right cars and teams to be with.

'They're also nice, genuine guys. George still wears his BRDC badge on his overalls' lapel. He's repaying what we tried to do for him. Lando will send me WhatsApps. He wasn't very happy with me in Austria when I gave him a five-second penalty. We've had a few discussions on that.

'But again, the funny thing about that is that when he came off the rostrum, they came into the stewards' room, to change his clothes or something – I can't remember. You come off the rostrum, and he's walking along the hallway, I'm stood there, and he looked at me and he gave me the stare, like, what the f**k? And then he gave me a fist pump. And I gave him the fist pump back, then he gave me the finger! Funny.

'I think they're very smart kids. They're very fit. They've got good people around them, they're well grounded. Super, super fast. And they know how to be racing drivers. You know, George is being patient at the minute, but Bahrain in 2020 showed us what he can do. He's going to be stunning in a Mercedes in 2022. He will learn a lot in the first year or two with Lewis. I won't say he will beat Lewis but he will on occasions. But he is gonna have a tough job ahead.

'And Lando – the world is his oyster. He's signed a longish-term contract, I think, with McLaren. Who's going to be there in another couple of years? Are they going to threaten Red Bull, Ferrari, and Mercedes genuinely? No. So he's gonna have a couple of tough, tough years. I suspect it depends how their 2022 car is compared to everybody else, but you just can't imagine that they're ever going to get back to the heights of where they were. So Lando is gonna have a bit of character building in the next couple of years if that car's not winning, because he deserves to be winning.'

Have you got any good stories from sitting in the stewards' room?
'No, unfortunately, it's a serious place to be. And obviously, anything you say in the stewards' room is in confidence. There was one thing which happened in Austria, which was funny. Kimi came together, right at the end of the race, with Seb [Vettel] – 100 per cent Kimi's fault but when he came into the room, he wasn't sure of that. He came for another incident earlier in the race when George moved under braking. The Chairman said, "You can stay here and wait for Seb. We've called for Vettel over the incident when you crashed at the end of the race." He sat there and never said anything. Then he just started talking about motor racing in general and how he'd love to have been racing in our day, not his day.

'Then he started talking about the incident. He said to me, "Did I turn right into Seb?" Yeah. "What, actually turned right?" Yeah. "So it was my fault?" Yeah – but we're gonna have to see because we've got the video. "Can I see the video?"

'I said, "No, you can't really see the video because Seb's not here."

'"Can I just have a little look at the video?" in his broad accent.

'So we showed him a clip of the video and, sure enough, he just turned right and drove into Seb. So when Seb comes in, Seb sits down and the Chairman says, "Right, OK guys, we'll just talk about your incident at the end of the race." Kimi just stands up and says, "Guilty – no point in talking about it. I'm guilty. My fault." It was funny because it was Kimi, Kimi being honest.

'Some drivers coming to the stewards' room will talk non-stop, trying to talk themselves out of the incident, even when they're bang to rights. Seb is a very good person at this – he will try everything to change your mind, even when I think he knows he's in the wrong.

'One of the smartest guys that comes into our stewards' room is Carlos [Sainz]. He's very articulate, he's very smart, and he remembers every millimetre of that particular incident. Whereas you've got other drivers that wouldn't even remember which race they were at!'

LANDO NORRIS

Interviewed by **DAVID TREMAYNE**

LANDO NORRIS (GB)
Born 13 November 1999

After a successful career in karting, Norris switched to cars in the 2014 Ginetta Junior Championship. The following year, he moved into single-seaters with Carlin Motorsport, contesting the new MSA Formula Championship. Having won that title, Norris did likewise in Formula Renault 2.0 and the European Formula Three Championship, and then finished third in the 2018 Formula Two Championship. A junior driver with McLaren since 2017, he was promoted to Formula One in 2019 alongside Carlos Sainz. He scored his first points in Bahrain that year, then posted his maiden podium finish at the 2020 Austrian Grand Prix.

Of all the drivers you have raced against in your career, which ones stood out for you?
'Carlos Sainz, because he's the first proper Formula One driver I got to work with. He's an extremely good driver and seeing both how he works and actually working alongside him helped me a lot. I think he's very good in all areas and so he was a good example.'

Which were the best teammates?
'I haven't had one "best" teammate. Every teammate I've had I've got along with since the very beginning. I've had many teammates but one of the best has been Colton Herta, who I raced alongside in British F4 and now he's in INDYCAR. He's a very good driver and one of the first single-seater teammates that I had. He's gone on to do really great things and we were really good mates when he was living in the UK.'

Who were the most difficult to work with, and why?
'I don't think I've ever had someone who's difficult to work with. Me and Sérgio Sette Câmara were two very different personalities. We worked together very well, and he was an extremely good teammate and very good driver, but how he went about things was very different to how I'd do things. He's very good in a lot of ways and I did learn a lot from him. He was a very different teammate to what I've been used to, but in a good way.'

Which driver do you think was the best of all time, and why?
'I have no opinion here. If it was a rider, not a driver, it would be Valentino Rossi!'

Who did you have the most fun with?
'Every year I've had a lot of fun and a lot of memories from every single season. One of the perks of junior categories is that you often have more than one teammate, so you all get along and create memories with the three or four of you. Between my Formula 4, Three and One teammates, Formula 4 was good with Colton Herta. We got along well and he's a funny guy. In Formula Three there were several: Jake Dennis, Jehan Daruvala, Sacha Fenestraz, Ferdinand Habsburg, Devlin DeFrancesco and Ameya Vaidyanathan, and some of us had been good mates since karting, so we had a lot of good laughs together.
'Formula One with Carlos because he's just a very normal, nice guy and we share similar interests, like golf. We both want to have a fun and enjoyable time and work hard within Formula One. We have a lot of similarities and that's why we got along so well.'

Who would you say is the bravest driver you've raced against?
'Colton Herta – he's a hooligan, that guy!'

Do you have any favourite amusing stories about fellow drivers?
'I have many, but I don't want to share them because a lot of them are embarrassing for them! I'm sure they have a lot of bad ones about me too, so I don't want to expose them otherwise karma will bite me. I do have many, but none I'm willing to share.'

What has been the biggest disappointment in your career?
'Winning everything bar Formula Two.'

A strong 2021 season for McLaren included Norris taking pole position here at Sochi for the Russian GP. (Motorsport Images)

EMERSON FITTIPALDI

Interviewed by **DAVID TREMAYNE**

EMERSON FITTIPALDI (BRA)
Born 12 December 1946

The battles between Jackie Stewart and Emerson Fittipaldi defined Formula One in the early 1970s, with Stewart winning the World Championship in 1971 and 1973 – to go with his first title in 1969 – and 'Emmo' doing likewise in 1972 and 1974. The first of Fittipaldi's titles came with Lotus, and at the time he was the sport's youngest World Champion. He then joined McLaren for the 1974 season, but left at the end of the following year to join his brother's new team. It proved to be a disaster, but Fittipaldi later rebuilt his career in America and twice won the Indy 500.

World Champion, Indianapolis 500 winner, CART Champion – Fittipaldi is without doubt a legend of the sport. (Steve Havelock)

Who was your best teammate?
'I always had very good teammates in Formula One and later in America, but the one I most enjoy working with together, because he was already a friend before, was Ronnie Peterson. Ronnie, to me, was the best. We were racing Formula Three and Formula Two together before Formula One, so I was always a very good friend of Ronnie. Barbro, his wife, is a friend of Maria-Helena's [Emerson's then wife]. He used to come to my house in Switzerland. I used to go to see him in England and it was always a great relationship, and when we were at Lotus together in 1973 it was fantastic to work with Ronnie – even when we were both in competition with each other.'

Who was the guy you looked to as being your greatest opposition?
'Well, you know I was lucky to race so many great drivers, but when I arrive in Formula One and then in 1972, for sure, was Jack Stewart. He was the biggest one, and then was Niki [Lauda] and many other guys too.
'So in the years with Lotus and McLaren, I always had incredible competition for sure, great drivers – but Jack was outstanding to me.'

Do you have a driver that you regard as the best of all time, the greatest?
'You know, my hero before I start racing was Fangio, and then with the modern racing, for sure, I loved Senna, but that's a little biased being Brazilian! When he started racing go-karts, I was a very good friend of the family, the father, everybody.'

And you said when you were racing, Jackie and Niki were the two best?
'If you look in the history of my days, was for sure Jack and Niki. But one time it was Clay [Regazzoni]. [Jacky] Ickx was very good. Carlos Reutemann was very fast. I mean, the cars at that time were extremely fast. There were so many good drivers at that time. I raced with Alain Prost and Mansell when they had just started. Nigel was extremely fast. John Watson was always very fast and consistent. So many good drivers, you know.'

What is it do you think that made the great ones really great? Could you ever define that?
'I think the great drivers were the ones that even when the car was not the best, they would carry it on their back and make an incredible performance with a bad car. I remember in 1973, Jack Stewart driving in Interlagos. His Tyrrell was so difficult to drive, but he was there. I mean, really strong the whole race. I won, but he finished second. And then at the end of the year he won the Championship... That was a good exhibition of talent, of being a great driver.'

Was there anyone out there that you were wary of racing wheel-to-wheel with?
'Yes – Clay [Regazzoni]! It was always dangerous to be close to Clay. I was afraid. I had a few bad experiences – when I say bad, I mean scary experiences – with Clay. Remember Watkins Glen in 1974, when I was trying to lap him when we were fighting for the Championship? That was a tough time, a very tough time. In Formula Two with him I had a few occasions as well, but that's history. But he was a great friend. I liked him, but on the track... [laughs].
'There were some drivers who were not the greatest champions. But with all the extremely talented drivers, I never had a problem.'

Was there anyone that stood out as being the bravest?
'Vittoria Brambilla, I think, was a very brave driver.'

What about Gilles Villeneuve?
'[Emerson smiles] Gilles was incredible. I remember when he first drove the McLaren in practice at Silverstone in 1977. I remember that he spun seven times, his first time in a Formula One car. It must be the world's record of spinning on your first time!'

Fittipaldi, JPS-liveried Lotus 72, Stewart and shades – such was the style of early 1970s Formula One. The two great champions were good friends. (Motorsport Images)

What about drivers who you got on with socially?

'Jochen [Rindt] was always very good to me. The first time in Nürburgring for the Formula Two race, I was in a Lotus and qualified fourth. I asked him, "Jochen, if I get into second at the start, can I follow you?" He said, "Yes." And I did get into second and I did follow Jochen, and the first lap everything Jochen was doing, I was doing. And I was thinking, "Great! The first lap, and I am second behind Jochen!"

'Then, when we were behind the pits, going downhill on the second lap, he just waved, "Bye, Emerson!" I lost the compass, I lost the GPS! He just disappeared. I finished fourth and afterwards I said, "Jochen, I still have a lot to learn!"

'Later, he helped me a lot when I first tested the Lotus 49C at Silverstone. And the morning he was killed, we had agreed a deal for me to drive for his Formula Two team in 1971…

'I always had a lot of great times with Jack Stewart, even today. I've always liked Jack a lot outside of the car. I also had very good relationship with Mario Andretti, who I also raced in America. He was a very good friend always. The Unser family in America, too, because of course I had two stages of my racing life – one in Europe and then later over there.

'In Formula One, the French drivers were like a group of their own. All the French journalists and the French drivers were always together, but I always had good times with them. François [Cevert] was another great guy.

'I think back then there was a respect to show each other because of the high risk we had, and every time we were outside of the cockpit we want to have fun. And one of the funniest when I had a great time was "Mike the Bike" [Mike Hailwood], for sure. Mike was a character, was always fun, and he did so many good drives. And like I said, Ronnie [Peterson] and I always had good fun, from Formula Three all the way to Formula One. We always exchanged good jokes, had good laughs. I liked Ronnie a lot.

'I don't know, there was a different relationship outside of the cockpit in those days. It was different from now. Maybe we were like soldiers back then, you know, facing danger all the time? Now everything is not the same if drivers make a mistake with an accident, thankfully, but it's the stress they face that is changing the sport. You don't have the same relationships as we used to.'

Did you have any favourite circuits?

'The old Nürburgring was number one! And then the old Interlagos, when there was five miles. It was bumpy, but it was very fast. And it was beautiful to do one perfect lap there, because Interlagos was difficult, very tough. And I love Brands Hatch, which is a very great track.'

Tell us about the Copersucar project. Why did you do that, and did you ever regret it or was it just a necessary part of your life?

'No, no regrets. It was part of my life, a big challenge. I had big support from Embraer, the aeroplane company, to develop a car in Brazil. It was very difficult to do the car there, but then in [my] last year [as a driver] we had a fantastic team. We had Keke Rosberg as my teammate, Peter Warr as team manager, Harvey Postlethwaite as the chief designer and Adrian Newey was a junior engineer. It was incredible. We had a very good new car running strong, but then we lost the sponsorship.

'It was a shame, but it was a great experience. It was myself, my brother Wilson. It was a big challenge, it was difficult, but it's from the most difficult and bad experiences in life that you learn a lot. I certainly learnt a lot from that!'

DEREK BELL

Interviewed by **PHILIP PORTER**

DEREK BELL (GB)
Born 31 October 1941

Derek Bell is one of the greatest sports car drivers of all time. He was twice World Sports Car Champion, won the Le Mans 24 Hours five times, and the Daytona 24 Hours three times. He is most closely associated with Porsche, and drove the 917 for the Gulf-JW Automotive team in the early 1970s, as well as the 956 and 962 during the IMSA and Group C heyday of the 1980s. Before any of that, he was a works Ferrari driver in single-seaters. His first Grand Prix was for the Scuderia in 1968 – at Monza, too – and he also raced for Enzo in Formula Two and the Tasman series. An enduring talent, he finished third at Le Mans as late as 1995.

Who would you say were your best teammates?

'That's not too difficult because it has to be the ones I had the greatest success with [laughing]. And I will say to start with, I was so fortunate, basically all my career, to have driven for the best teams in the world and therefore we had the best teammates. I wouldn't say I manoeuvred my way into being in the best seat but I wanted to be with the best guy in the team, if I could – but I never said anything. My driving, I guess, generally allowed me to get into a good position.

'Starting in chronological order, it would be Jacky Ickx, because he was really my first teammate. I met him at Ferrari doing Formula Two, as I did, plus Chris Amon. And then of course, we did Formula One together. But that's a different sort of teammate; I am really talking about when you shared with a driver. I met Jacky and had this incredible respect for him because he was three years or so younger than me. I was 27; he was 24. And he was a star. I still to this day would say that he should have been a Formula One World Champion.

'He was outstandingly good; he had such a talent; he had such a mentality. He was never any bother; he got on with the job. He very rarely crashed. And he made a wonderful teammate for me. He was also versatile. When I drove with him in those early years, he had already driven Mustangs, Formula Three, Formula Two and Formula One. I had too, but I was two years later than him, although he was younger.

'So he set the benchmark for what I came to expect of myself. When Jacky left Ferrari, Chris became a very close friend of mine. But he and Jacky were great teammates. And it seemed like there was competitiveness between them. But really, the challenge, particularly in Formula One in those days, was not necessarily to beat your teammates to prove how good you were, it was to beat the cars in the other teams. That's where I think it's gone a bit astray in car racing throughout the world — everyone is comparing you to your teammates.

'I'm not saying you shouldn't race – we raced like hell. And there were two of us driving in those days [in endurance racing], not three or even four. So it was tremendously competitive, but I was never trying to beat Jacky. I was always trying to be as quick as him.

'I was thrown into the Ferrari team at Le Mans, and they put me with Ronnie Peterson and we drove the 512. He and I had never been to Le Mans before. We were all so damn new to it that we went around with our mouths wide open.

'He was bloody quick, very quick. The next year I was in the 917. Ronnie and I had had the test drive together at Goodwood with Peter Gethin, in September 1970, and somehow I got the drive. I'm not sure to this day why. I think Ronnie was quicker than me but he was less experienced. I don't think he had beaten me in Formula Two, but he was a hot-shoe at that point.

He had a great reputation in Formula One, didn't he?

'That's right. But he was always sideways. It was brilliant to watch. It was wonderful racing against him; never had any moments with him. Peter Gethin was the other driver who was going for the drive in the John Wyer Porsche. Peter was much more my sort of pace, my level of ability. He would probably argue, if he was alive, that he was quicker!'

What was Ronnie Peterson like as a person?

'He was great; he was so laid back. He had such a great sense of humour. We had many laughs. Three or four years later, we were racing at Watkins Glen, and there was me and Niki Lauda and Ronnie Peterson doing the Grand Prix and we just had so many laughs together. It was tense in the cars, but I think that's why, when you were out of the cars, it was such a relief to be out of these death traps.

'With Ronnie we had many, many laughs and unfortunately some of the stories I can't repeat. All the guys stayed at the Kyalami Ranch Hotel [in South Africa], whether it was sports cars or Formula One. There were two airlines – Sabena Air and Alitalia – and the crews used to stay at the same hotel at this resort. And you can imagine: there's a load

Bell drifting the Ferrari 312 at the 1968 Oulton Park Gold Cup. It was while driving for the Scuderia that he first met Jacky Ickx. (Motorsport Images)

of very healthy, fit-looking Formula One or sports car drivers, and about three dozen beautiful girls from all over the world. It was an awful situation for us all! We wondered what we were there for...'

How about Jo Siffert, who was also part of that Gulf-JW Automotive team?
'I wouldn't say I was close to Jo Siffert as I only did five races with him. He was as quick as anybody in the world. Pedro [Rodríguez] wouldn't have agreed, but he was. He and Pedro were on a par. They were different in so many ways but excellent drivers. I never shared with Pedro, unfortunately. I once did a very good time at Spa in qualifying and out-qualified Jackie Oliver in the other car, and Jo and Pedro. I did a 161mph lap in qualifying on the old Spa in that bloody car, which is one of the quickest laps probably ever at any track in the world. I'd never thought about it until somebody sent me the lap times about five or 10 years ago and I've got them all printed out in every room I walk into just to check I really did do it!

'I had caught up Oliver in the race but they wouldn't allow me to overtake. Jo had done his bit and Pedro was in the lead, and in fact it was our turn to win at Spa. After the race, Pedro came up to me and he liked that I'd caught Oliver and if they'd allowed me to overtake I was going to do so, but they just kept putting a board out saying, "Hold". For an hour and a half they stuck this sodding board out. I had proved that I was quicker in practice.

Bell and Jo Siffert were a regular pairing at Gulf-JW Automotive during the 1971 season. This is Brands Hatch, where they were third. (Motorsport Images)

'Nonetheless Ollie was brilliant, I'm not saying he wasn't, but I was better around there and we laugh about it to this day. Every time he sees me, he says, "Who won at Spa?"

'Anyway, he never missed a gear, never put a damn foot wrong, and I was pushing, pushing. David Yorke [team manager] was putting the board out saying "Hold position" and then 50 yards further around the corner was Siffert [waving his arms] going, "Come on, come on – overtake him."

'"Seppi" would have overtaken him but I was only in my third race [for the team] and I was used to public school and the headmaster, and John Wyer was the bloody headmaster and so I obeyed him – and I'm glad I did, really.

'After that race I remember Pedro was sitting there eating, as he used to, very hot chilli peppers: "Derek, I think it [sic] time you drive with me now," and he ate another pepper! That was nice but then, of course, he died so that was the end of that – and then Jo died. When you look at it, it was tragic when both your teammates died in that one year.'

Brian [Redman] told me that Siffert was quite a fun guy and started a food fight on one occasion by flicking some butter across the room at somebody.

'I don't remember that but I do remember when we were testing at Hockenheim in October or November 1970 and "Seppi" went off the road and crashed, and the car was in pieces. So everybody rushes out to find him, and when they get there they can't find him. The car's just all over the road and he's hiding behind the guardrails and suddenly pops his head up and says, "Hey, I'm here!"

'He was that sort of bloke. He's just destroyed a car worth a bloody fortune but that was Jo. He did really funny things like that and we had some good times together.

'They were the halcyon days for racing: dangerous but the guys were great. We had so many bloody good drivers – people like Ronnie Peterson and Chris Amon, Pedro, Jimmy Clark at times, and Graham Hill, Jackie Stewart. It was incredible when you think about it.'

And Jochen Rindt?
'Jochen Rindt, of course.'

Why was he so good in Formula Two?
'In reality, he was so good in anything. I was in my first season in F2 in 1970 and we were invariably running first and second, but I could not beat him. A newspaper in Belgium would call him "la roi" [the king] and I was "le dauphin" [the heir]. I beat him in one race and that was in New Zealand.'

I have been told he could be quite aggressive on the track.
'I never saw that. He was just bloody good. He was like Ronnie – they were always broadside and sliding. It was gorgeous to watch and I was wondering if I had to drive like that. I never did really drive like that and I wouldn't necessarily have the car set up to drive like that.

'They just had that extra something, that strong quality. They were amazing. I got to know Jochen really well because I did the Tasman series at the end of 1968 and beginning of '69 with Chris Amon when we were driving for Ferrari in the Dinos.

'What a fantastic series. There were two Lotuses for Graham [Hill] and Jochen, and Piers Courage in the Frank Williams Brabham. It was just a lovely group and we had seven races, four in New Zealand and three in Australia. We had such camaraderie. I got to know them all so well because we had breakfast, lunch and dinner together. It was fantastic and drivers don't have that these days.'

Was Graham Hill great fun?
'Oh God, he was a riot – he was such a character but he was wise. In the last race in New Zealand, Jochen and Chris were on the front row and I was on the second alongside Piers, with Graham behind me. It was two by two by two because it was so narrow, and then behind Graham was, I guess, somebody like Frank [Gardner] because there were a lot of local drivers that had good cars, knew the tracks and had them set up for the tracks.

'I remember sitting on the grid and there was no room. I mean, we were just packed in there. Of course they were standing starts. I'll never forget, they dropped the flag and Jochen, right in front of me, moved about six feet. When I saw him spin the wheels, I had let my clutch out, being a bit excited and wanting to get on with the show. And unfortunately, I then hit him in the back. The reason was, his driveshaft had broken. So I hit him in the back, that moved him forward and I thought, "Oh, he's off again." Then I went over his rear wheel and we were all "bang, bang" – everybody hits everybody.

'That night at the prizegiving, Graham said to me, "If I had let the clutch out when you did, we would have had a mighty crash." He said, "You don't move until the car in front moves." Graham was so wise and I've always remembered that.'

Are you able to compare Jackie Stewart and Jimmy Clark and Graham Hill?
'I raced against Graham a lot. I could never decide between Jackie and Jimmy. There was something about Jimmy – he was just a little bit quicker. But it might have been on certain occasions, and of course he might have been in a better car. I'd hate to say.

Bell pictured with Brian Redman (centre) and Steve McQueen during filming of *Le Mans*. McQueen had some eye-opening moments on set. (Motorsport Images)

Who had more accidents? I think Jimmy had a cleaner career until tragically the race, which I was in with him, when he died. To me, he was the complete racing driver. Don't get me wrong, I think Jackie was amazing. Probably underrated.'

You did a lot of filming with Steve McQueen for the film Le Mans. How good a driver was he?
'He was, I think, a lot better than we all thought. At that time, 1970, I'd been racing for just five years and I wasn't really an expert on who had talent and who hadn't. I had a pretty meteoric rise from Formula Three to Formula One in the space of two years, but I wasn't a good judge of people's driving skills, because it all happened too fast. So during that year we did the movie – we started that in June-July.

'Steve drove with us, but of course I wouldn't get in the same car as him ever. With Jo Siffert, we did a lot of shooting together and he would drive Steve's car or else he would drive the second Porsche. I was always in the Ferrari. We knew you shouldn't go too fast, because we didn't want to blow the cars up, we didn't want to damage anything. And how well were they prepared? People got pretty nonchalant: "That car's prepared." Well, what's this pool of fuel under the car on the floor that might go up in flames at any time?

'So preparation wasn't incredibly good. But nonetheless, Steve did drive with us a lot and he was driving a 917. I never saw him driving a Ferrari but the 917 was an easier car to drive. In a way, anyone could drive a 917. You get in the Ferrari, and it's very clunky. I always said that when I drove the 512 it was a bit like driving a truck. But the 917 was very driver-friendly, although if you put your foot down, you could spin the wheels and go out of control. So Steve, fortunately for him, was driving that. I never heard of him having any accident. If he had an accident while we made the movie, we'd have known about it because he would have got hurt – you don't have a crash in a 917 without getting hurt.

'I always had respect for him. On one occasion when we finished a shot, I'd kept my foot in it because I was getting a bit bored of going through White House seven or eight times. On the seventh time, I just didn't back off as much and Steve being Steve hung on. We then all jumped out of our cars waiting for the director at the Ford Chicane and, I'll never forget it, Steve was as white as a sheet. And he said, "What happened there? That stupid bastard Derek just went through the corners nearly flat out." I said, "You didn't have to follow me. You could have backed off if you didn't like it." He didn't, he kept his foot in it and he didn't have a moment but it did frighten him. So, I think he was very good.

'He drove my Formula Two Brabham on the Bugatti track [at Le Mans]. We were on our way to a race somewhere in central France, and leading the Championship. But he didn't push it; he drove very modestly. And then I realised that he was 10 years older than me: I was 30, he was 40. Although he had raced various cars, I didn't realise how many because he just didn't talk about that sort of thing. But he drove that F2 car with respect. Some guys would have gotten in that and driven the s**t out of it and risked spinning off. But he didn't. He had respect for the car, understood racing and that it was my car.

'We would only do sections of laps [during filming], you've got to realise. If we did a run on the Mulsanne Straight, we'd only use part of it. They'd shut it off [to the public] so we could run there for two hours and we'd come out of Tertre Rouge, and go down there nose to tail. I had that frigging great camera, stuck out on a boom out the side. And when it swung in, it put the car up in the air – the whole nose lifted from the weight of it. That is why I drove and not Steve, that's when I used to stand in for him on things like that. Some of the stuff we did wasn't easy – you had to be a racing driver to do it because you had to be able to judge whether it was safe or not.'

Talking of making judgements, who do you think was the bravest driver you competed against or with?
'I would think without a doubt it was Stefan Bellof.'

That's what everybody says!
'Yes. But I don't know that he was brave. I really adored that boy. He used to call me father and I used to call him son. And we were really close. He was just a cracking kid, and terribly talented, but had no idea of the limit. He was quicker than me because he did, no doubt, have superior ability. He was also 20 years younger and he had balls of steel, but he didn't really realise the limits.

'We were at the Nürburgring and I'd never won any race, ever, at the Nürburgring. I'd come second, I'd been on pole in every class of racing except for Formula One. I'd even finished two Grands Prix there but I'd never won. I'd been leading when things would go wrong. I love it but couldn't win at the sodding place. I could win at Le Mans five times – I'd happily give up a Le Mans win for a Nürburgring 1,000km win.

'So, we were there for the 1,000km. The fact was, we knew Stefan was quicker; we knew he was braver. He was 25 and I was 42. And they knew that he was the one that was going to get an outrageous lap, not me. I mean, I'm not stupid, and they're not stupid. So as sure as eggs is eggs, they put on a special set of tyres. And allowed him possibly to use more revs, I don't know, but they would do all these things

Bell has become a respected ambassador for motor racing, and his long career brought him into contact with many of the sport's other greats. (Michael Cole)

to get him pole. I'm convinced those sorts of things happened. Because when I look back on it, I remember certain things being said, which made you believe, "Hello, he's got something special here." And I don't begrudge him that at all.

'I remember during that race we were leading by, I don't know, three to four minutes. Remember, I'd never won at that damn track. And he started to go even quicker. It's easy to do that – to go quicker every lap – if you're given the freedom to do it. I walked up to the head of the team, and I won't mention names, and I just said, "Why don't we put a board out with HOLD? Isn't it time to steady him down? There's still an hour and a half to go. I want to win the f*****g race, do you mind?"

'This particular person turned to me and said, "Isn't he marvellous?" That was it. And Stefan never came around the next lap…

'He didn't get hurt but he damaged the car considerably. I think he should have had more guidance from his teams. John Wyer would instruct his drivers: "This is what I want you to do." He was a good manager, good boss; he knew your limits. And he would have known that if Bellof could do a 1-41, "Then Derek you do 1-42. We'll be really happy with that." But they never told him anything, they never held him back.

'That incident when he crashed [fatally] at Spa: I saw an in-car camera from behind Jacky's head in the cockpit and he kept on the line perfectly the whole way around Spa. Now the fact that Bellof was trying to get past him going into the bottom turn at Eau Rouge is lunacy. You don't overtake anybody there because it's a left-hander into right into another left, and you couldn't get two cars up there in those days with the grip we had. All right, they might do it now. They've moved the fences back, they've opened it all up. And you can go two abreast because all the cars have so much grip, but our bloody things were dancing around like a headless bitch. Why did Jacky go out of control? Because he was hit by Bellof. Why would Stefan do that? He had so much time out there to get him on the next lap.

'He was probably running more power because he was in a private team. So he was probably running 50 horsepower more

The Bell/Stuck/Holbert Porsche 962 on its way to victory at the 1986 Le Mans 24 Hours – the fourth of Bell's five wins in the great race. (Ian Wagstaff)

because it was so exciting for the team to run like that. I'm not blaming Stefan. I am blaming him for his own crash, yes, because I saw the in-car twice for two laps and Jacky kept a perfect line, everywhere. Two guys nearly got killed because of that silly move.

'I always felt that Ken Tyrrell and Porsche, basically, would have slowed him down. They would have said, "This kid's got talent. Let's nurture it and bring him on to be something great."

'Often in these races, Stefan would be lapping in incredible times, the car would come in and I get in it and off. I'd be building up speed and getting up to pace. And suddenly they put a board out or call me and say, "Turn the boost down, turn the fuel mixture down, and drop your revs from eight-five to eight-two." Why was that, do you think? Because he'd used too much friggin' fuel. So DB had to slow down. Then the journalists are going, "Derek Bell's not very quick." That's the back story.

'Of all the drivers in sports cars, he was the quickest, but he really wasn't the safest.'

Were there any female racing drivers that you respected, you felt were quick and should be there on merit?

'I think Desiré Wilson was bloody good. I don't think she ever drove the right cars. I think she drove a 962 a couple of times. It's very difficult for somebody to say, "Desiré, come and drive our car at Le Mans." If you haven't driven the car all year, you're not going to be as good as us lot in the Rothmans. Now, if somebody at Rothmans had thought about it and said, "Let's put her in a third car along with Al Holbert and Hurley Haywood", I think she would have done OK, but she wasn't driving 962s every week. I think Desiré was bloody good.

'I remember I drove in Formula One [the Shellsport International Series] against Divina Galica at Donington and I think my gear lever broke so I was having to use the stub, and not finding it very easy to drive. She beat me into fourth place or something. I remember thinking, "God, I was beaten by a girl!" which is awful because she was so good. She taught [my son] Justin how

The one that got away – Hans Stuck pictured at Le Mans in 1988, when he and Bell, with Klaus Ludwig, finished a close second. (Motorsport Images)

to ski in the Alps and she was in the British team, and I always admired her and liked her immensely. The car she drove was never the best. Tyrrell wasn't going to put Divina in a car if he could put Stefan Bellof in, simply because it's going to take too long for her to get up to speed.'

What are your memories of James Hunt?
'I went to his first wedding when he married Suzy, at Brompton Oratory. It was a lovely wedding. He was such a character; we knew each other for years because we were both British. We ultimately drove together in the Mirage, or actually he drove the Mirage and then he refused to drive it anymore. I had to get in because Mike Hailwood had crashed our car, so I didn't really get to know him

> *'And Jochen said to me, "When you have to risk your life to get on the grid, there's something wrong with the car."'*

racing-wise, but he was very, very good. He enjoyed it. I mean James was James, and what you read about him is what he was like. There was no bulls***ting. But he was very quick.

'One heard that he was sat on the grid at Monaco for his last Grand Prix in tears because he was so frightened. I can't believe that that's the case. But it makes a story for somebody to write and people to read about because they're always looking for weakness.

'James was so good for the sport because of the playboy image that he had. He was fantastic. The likes of Michael Schumacher come along and the only way Michael was going to be famous was by winning the World Championship seven times and being so dominant, and he was in a Ferrari. Sports are made up of characters, aren't they?'

How about Mike Hailwood? He was another character.
'What a character. You've got Surtees, and then you've got Hailwood. Surtees – how can anybody like Surtees not get knighted? When you see people getting knighted for winning Wimbledon, and there is John Surtees who was [motorcycle] World Champion seven times and then won the Formula One World Championship as well, and in a Ferrari. I mean, Jesus, what's the guy got to do?'

He upset people, didn't he?
'Well, that's it. But isn't that wrong? It's meant to be a measure of his ability. He never upset me, but I heard the stories. But that was John. That's why he got to where he got. I remember driving for him. I got my only World Championship point with sixth place in the United States Grand Prix in 1970.

'John was amazing and he was an engineer. He was a pain in the arse as an engineer. But he was always underfunded and had to use old engines. I drove for him again in '73 and '74 in a number of races, and we could hardly qualify.

'It was me and Jochen Mass and we were at the British Grand Prix. He and I were 35th and 36th in practice. And Jochen said to me, "When you have to risk your life to get on the grid, there's something wrong with the car." For the first race of the year, Carlos Pace had been on the front row at Kyalami with the same car; four months later, we're at the back of the grid.

'Now, if it had just been me, I'd have said, "Well, I'm a bit of a w****r", but Jochen was pretty bloody good. He did well in Formula One. But that was the way John was. I remember coming back from those races and, when I got together with a mechanic, he literally wrote my comments on the back of a cigarette packet about what we should do to the car. It was a shambles. And he wasn't happy with me, or with any of us, unless we could go quickly.

'I was so sad when he died. I used to do a lot of charity stuff with him and he and I got on well.'

We should talk about Hans Stuck.
'When I think of the great drivers that I drove with who left their mark, it was Jacky Ickx, Stefan Bellof and Hans Stuck, and then Al Holbert, the American driver. In reality, the two characters in my life in racing were Jacky Ickx and then Hans Stuck. Jacky doesn't have the character of "Stucky" but he has something about him that is astonishing.

'"Stucky" was just Hans Stuck. We drove together in Formula Three, in Formula Two and then, thank God, he came and drove with me at Porsche. He said to me that when he joined Porsche, Professor Bott said, "We're putting you with Derek Bell, because he might straighten you out and mature you and bring you on as a driver." He never crashed again. I didn't choose him the year before, when I was with Stefan Bellof, because I remember he kept having his moments, coming in with damaged cars. The reason was, he was trying too bloody hard to drive a heap of s**t, and not getting anywhere fast so he kept going off.'

What made him good? Was it car control?
'First of all, he had the natural talent of his father, who was such a great driver in the Auto Unions. Then you have his versatility with touring cars, sports cars… Whatever he drove, he was a joy to watch. I drove with him in the BMW team. Having driven against him in F2, it was really strange. I drove against him in F2 at Hockenheim and he sat on my tail for the whole bloody race in whatever he was in and then went by on the last lap. Afterwards he said, "Thank you so much. I learned so much by being behind you today."

'He was always a gentleman and very correct. That was lovely because no other driver ever said that to me in all my career. We instantly became friends and, of course, then I drove with him at BMW in the touring cars. I got to know "Stucky" really well and then he joined me with the Rothmans Porsche and he was just a fantastic teammate. He was a totally different person to Jacky Ickx but nonetheless, at the same time, he could turn on those electrifying quick laps and became very safe. So the two were very, very similar but different personalities. Jacky is the one that always stays in my memory because they were my formative years and his whole demeanour made me what I became in racing. Whereas with "Stucky", if anything, it loosened me up and made me have a good time.'

TIM PARNELL

Interviewed by **PHILIP PORTER** in 2006

TIM PARNELL (GB)
Born 25 June 1932
Died 5 April 2017

After a short-lived career as a driver in which he competed in sports cars, Formula Junior and even a handful of Grands Prix, Tim Parnell took over the running of the family team in 1964 following the death of his father – renowned former racer Reg Parnell. The privateer outfit ran BRMs, Lolas and Lotuses for the likes of Chris Amon, Richard Attwood and Piers Courage, and after it closed down Parnell ran the works BRM team. It was under his stewardship that the Bourne equipe won its last four Championship Grands Prix courtesy of Pedro Rodríguez, Jo Siffert, Peter Gethin and Jean-Pierre Beltoise.

Opposite page, top: Parnell dices with the UDT-Laystall Lotus 18 of Henry Taylor during the 1961 Lombank Trophy at Snetterton. (Motorsport Images)

Which drivers were best at overcoming challenging conditions?

'My father [Reg Parnell] was ever so good at adapting to things. He was brilliant in the rain and I used to say, "Why are you so good in the rain?" He said, "Because I can adapt to the conditions, and I take on the conditions. I don't let the conditions dictate to me." That's how Stirling [Moss] was as well. Whatever the conditions were, Stirling would adapt to them.

'So would Graham [Hill]. For the whole of one race at the Nürburgring he was dicing with John Surtees. The conditions were appalling but Graham took it on and dictated to it. He was going to win. Tremendous strength of character.'

Do you recall any high jinks?

'After the French GP at Reims, which was Champagne country, it used to flow like water. We used to have a wonderful reception in the town hall and then we always used to go to a bar round the corner.

'One year the bar was absolutely solid. We were so crushed you couldn't really put your hand out to pick up your drink. Anyway, *Madame* decided that some people had to go, and nobody wanted to go. So she sent for the police. They arrived and they tried to get some order restored.

'Trevor Taylor and I were jammed in this bar when these policemen got hold of us and threw us out of the door. The next minute there was gunfire – I think they were shooting in the air. Trevor and I set off down the road, thinking it was getting bloody serious. There were more shots and Trevor dived under a vehicle. The next moment a policeman pushed a gun into me and carted me off to the Black Maria [police van]. I got thrown in there. I remember David Piper sitting there with a glass in his hand – he'd been arrested as well.

'They slammed the back doors and we set off and there was an almighty crash – somebody had fastened the back bumper bar to a tree! More people were arrested and thrown into this vehicle. Then we set off again and we all finished up on the floor on one side. Some bright spark had undone the wheel nuts!

'By this time, the police were going barmy about this and we all got carted off down to the prison. There was banging on the doors and on the windows, and a big delegation of drivers and mechanics. Stan Elsworth, who had been a Vanwall mechanic, was saying, "Unless you release the prisoners, we are going to storm the jail." With that, they took us round the back and let us out and told us to clear off. I'm sure Graham [Hill] was there leading the rescue expedition.'

What was Graham Hill like to work with?

'He was a very tough man when it came to his racing. He required high standards of preparation and was very meticulous about what the mechanics had done and what they were doing. He made sure he got what he wanted in the car. Very, very strict; very tough to work with. A man who knew what he wanted, and went out to achieve what he needed to do.

'He did a heck of a lot of testing. He was one of these men who was obsessed with testing for long periods, and really tried everything. The only comparison I can make with all the drivers I worked with was Niki Lauda. He was the same. He'd sit in the car all day, testing and trying things and working things out – such dedication and devotion.

'Graham wasn't a natural like Jim Clark or Jackie Stewart but he worked so hard at it to get there.'

Would you have a good party after the Monaco Grand Prix?

'Graham [Hill] always made sure he went in the Tip Top Bar after Monte Carlo, and Rosie's Bar – Rosie was a great fan of Graham's. Of course, as soon as he appeared after the prizegiving, it would all take off. And the police would come down and try to restore order.

'We used to have straw bales in those days around the circuit. One year the straw bales outside the Tip Top Bar were set on fire. Well, there was hell to pay. All the fire engines and the police arrived – that was the end of straw bales at Monte Carlo! I think they were frightened the whole town would burn down. Oh, it was riotous!'

Can you recall an example of Graham's famous wit?
'I was with him once when he was giving a talk to the London School of Economics and some bright spark stood up and said, "Do you speak to your wife when having sex?"

'"It depends if there's telephone handy," he said. It caused one hell of an uproar.'

Was there great camaraderie in the 1960s?
'In the Tasman races we used to get 100 bottles of Champagne for the fastest lap in practice. Of course, that ensured we had magnificent parties afterwards. On one occasion, it looked as though Jack Brabham was going to win the Champagne and we said, "This can't happen because Jack isn't in our hotel." We were in the same hotel as Lotus and we said, "We'd better do something about this."

'So Graham and Jackie [Stewart] and Jim Clark went out and slip-streamed each other so we made sure we got the Champagne. The camaraderie in those days was phenomenal. Wonderful drivers, wonderful people, wonderful wives who all joined in.'

It sounds as if you have very special memories of Graham.
'Another thing I always remember about him was his magnificent attitude to his fellow drivers. When Jackie Stewart had his horrific crash at Spa [in 1966], which Graham had seen, he stopped and went down into the woodyard where Jackie had finished up. He helped to get Jackie out of the car because he was stuck in it. If the damn thing had caught fire, well, that would have been the end of Jackie Stewart. I'll always remember that great sacrifice to go and get his fellow teammate out of that car.

'I would honestly say that Graham was the greatest man I ever met, or was associated with, in motor racing. The things he did for the sport, the things he did for his fellow drivers, and the way he took the sport to the public. He gave such wonderful value to the public. Great, great man.'

Parnell (left) walks to the grid with Ireland, Moss and Clark at Silverstone in 1961. (Motorsport Images)

MARK WEBBER

Interviewed by **BEN EDWARDS**

MARK WEBBER (AUS)
Born 27 August 1976

Mark Webber started racing cars in 1994 and, having moved to the UK from his native Australia, secured a works Formula Ford drive with Van Diemen for 1996. He finished second in the British Championship, then graduated to F3 in 1997 with Alan Docking Racing, and at the end of that year he signed with Mercedes-Benz to race the CLK-GTR in the FIA GT Championship. He made his F1 debut in 2002 with Minardi, and after stints at Jaguar and Williams, he joined Red Bull in 2007. Between 2009 and 2012, and with Sebastian Vettel as a teammate, he won nine Grands Prix. After retiring from Formula One at the end of the 2013 season, he joined the Porsche sports car team and won the 2015 World Endurance Championship drivers' title.

'Multi 21, Seb.' A low point between teammates as Vettel ignores team orders and overtakes Webber in Malaysia, 2013. (Motorsport Images)

Which drivers were the best teammates you had?
'David [Coulthard] would certainly be up there because he taught me a lot. In a healthy way for me, he was on his way out, and obviously he had a lot of knowledge and a wealth of experience of how to handle lots of situations, and of developing a team too. We were doing that at Red Bull and I sort of had my tail between my legs a little bit after being at Williams, which was a tough period, and trying to reinvigorate my career. David was full of energy and had a wealth of knowledge, so we got on really, really well. It was only a short-term relationship, for a year, because David retired. But that was a very enjoyable relationship and I think highly professional.

'Sebastian and I had our absolute flashpoints, which were very well advertised, and certainly put a tremendous amount of friction in the relationship for a majority of it, but there were times also [when] we did get on quite well, which I think was, to be honest, the case for most of my teammates. Culturally, I think you get on better with the nationalities that you have more of a bias towards. I didn't really socialise with Nico Rosberg much, or actually even Sebastian, but of course I did with David. And I got on pretty well with Antonio Pizzonia.'

Was your relationship with Sebastian the most challenging?
'Absolutely. Everything made it challenging. I think it's easy as teammates to get on really easily when you're mid-pack. You've got a glue that needs to happen, whether it's engineering or whatever. You are fighting against everyone else, as a team, to get towards the front. And then when you are, when there's only two dogs left, and there's only one bowl of food, then it's an issue.

'So it really gets quite challenging when the victories start to come around, and the friction naturally builds from there. So we went on a journey. We couldn't believe that, off the back of DC's work and then Seb arrived, we sort of got the team in a position, with great recruitment through those years, where we could go and fight Ferrari and McLaren and Williams – all the big dogs. We thought, "Wow, we are finally doing this on our own terms."

'And then the internal battle starts and you find yourself having some challenges with engineering and driver friction and transparency, which then makes it more difficult. But that's Formula One – ultimately, there has to be some of that, there has to be some friction and needle. We've seen that every single time there's teammates on the front row together – then you've got to have friction.'

Would you say DC was the one you had the most fun with, the guy that you'd probably go to the pub with?
'By a mile. I met David for the first time in 2002, I think it was. We were on a plane together, just a British Airways flight from Nice to Heathrow, and I sat next to him. David was established and I was just in my first year of Formula One. I remember talking to him about helmets and all sorts. He had just a wealth of knowledge on the technical side, and the relationship just went from strength to strength, and with the GPDA [Grand Prix Drivers' Association] we just got on well. It was just a complete fluke we ended up as teammates, and also our relationship now is strong.

'He's definitely the driver that I've caught up with most socially, whether it's with his family barbecues or him coming here for our family barbecues or whatnot, we've had some good times.'

Were there any other drivers who weren't teammates that you ended up pretty close to?
'Yeah. Geographically it is a challenge with Rubens [Barrichello]. I always had a good relationship with Rubens. I went to his place in São Paulo. It was always good to see him. Jenson [Button] to a degree, yes.

'Of the younger guys, Max [Verstappen] has come to stay with me in Australia. So that's been enjoyable.

'I like to help the youngsters coming through now. It's interesting seeing these young bucks come through. You've only been retired for what seems like five minutes but it's now seven years since I've been in

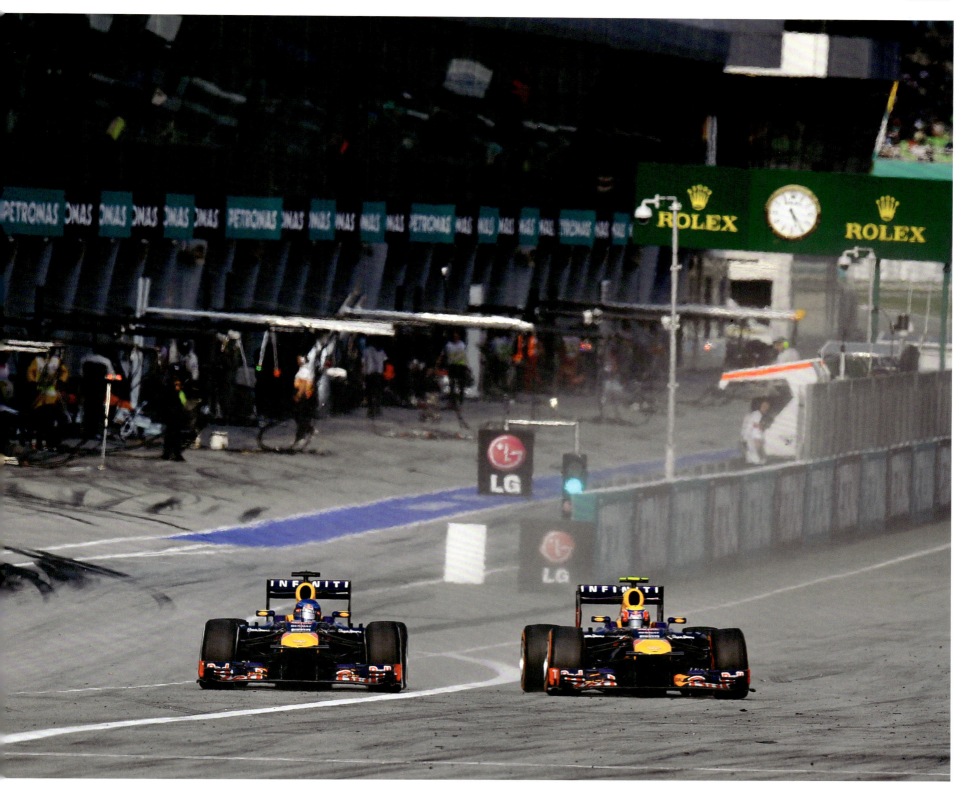

F1, so it goes so fast. I've got time now to show them Australia or show them a slice of something different, and that's enjoyable if you can have a bit of a relationship with them. I think the word is respect; we have a bit of a brotherhood. Culturally we get on well, and we can have a nice tennis match. It takes respect to have a good relationship and I think that when you have that then you enjoy hanging out together.'

I remember you telling me about when Max came and the guys on the beach were outdoing him.
'He is some true competitor and trivialised it at the start and then it was like, "Yeah OK, I could learn something here."
'Sports cars, that's another thing. That's what I'd class as the ultimate teammates and you get so, so close in sports car racing that that's another layer again.'

Who did you get closest to in sports car racing? Who did you work best with?
'Brendan [Hartley] and Timo [Bernhard]. We did so much together. We had so many great results together, so many tough moments – retiring at Le Mans when we were leading with 90 minutes to go. We were leading again in 2016 with a healthy lead and we had a water pump failure. I remember both times it was while I was driving at Le Mans. In the first year when we had the engine failure, for Brendon it was just the end of the world for him. It was literally the end of the world. I said, "Mate, you'll have opportunities, you're young…" I was talking him through it like that.
'I remember when Timo came to wake me up when we were leading, in the middle of the night. When you have those really heart-wrenching moments where the team put so much into it, and everyone's worked hard, there's no better person to hear it from than your teammate because you know the news, whether it's good or bad, you know they'll deliver it in a way which we can accept as best we can, and that bond gets closer. Then, when you have great moments, it's awesome because you really, really do have to work. It's insane. There's no cute funny business or politics, or you flush it out pretty quickly if there is. The car shouldn't know who's driving it; you need to [effectively] have one driver. The car really has to be operating as close as you can as one team.'

Interesting. That makes it a very different teammate relationship.
'Yeah, totally.'

So, in your era, who was the best?
'Michael [Schumacher]. Michael was at his peak, Lewis was not at his peak yet. So I had the junction of Michael finishing and Lewis starting. Looking back, having spent some time with those guys, not much wheel-to-wheel because they were disappearing, but I was very fortunate to race those guys a few times. And [I raced] Lewis more than Michael but it would naturally be those two.'

Riding the kerbs during the 2014 Spa Six Hours. Webber shared the Porsche 919 with Hartley and Bernhard. (Motorsport Images)

> 'There's no cute funny business or politics, or you flush it out pretty quickly if there is.'

ANDY WALLACE

Interviewed by **MARK COLE**

ANDY WALLACE (GB)
Born 19 February 1961

Now known as a legend of sports car racing, Wallace began his career in single-seaters and won the 1986 British Formula Three Championship. He tested for the Benetton Formula One team and moved up to Formula 3000 before joining the TWR-Jaguar sports car outfit in 1988. That year, and at his first attempt, he won the Le Mans 24 Hours alongside Jan Lammers and Johnny Dumfries. He added three victories in the Daytona 24 Hours (1990, 1997 and 1999), plus two at the Sebring 12 Hours (1992 and 1993), and at the time of writing he is an ambassador for Bugatti.

Of all the drivers you raced against in your career, which ones stood out for you in each decade?

'In the 1980s, it was Jan Lammers, my teammate when I won Le Mans in 1988 and Daytona in 1990, both for Jaguar. His car control, his way of analysing race strategy and his driving in general put him at the top for me. He was the complete driver; he had been tutored by Rob Slotemaker, the Dutch skid king, from about the age of seven!

'In the 1990s, it was James Weaver, my long-time teammate in America – a very, very complete driver. There are a lot of people I could fit in that box, but James was a safe pair of hands, always fast. He was one of those people who would always do what was necessary to win.

'He was as good off track as he was on, one of the guys, generous in setting up the car, not just the way he wanted it, but how you both wanted it.

'We won Daytona together in 1997. That was the year we all piled in when our Dyson car broke early. After a good night's sleep, James and I came back to the track to find the sister car still leading, but everyone totally exhausted, and being beaten up by the Momo Ferrari 333 SP. So we took over from Rob Dyson, Elliott Forbes-Robinson, Butch Leitzinger, John Paul Jr and John Schneider. There were seven of us on the top step of the podium; there weren't enough winners' Rolexes to go round!

'In the 2000s, it was still James, but I would bring Butch Leitzinger into that. We raced at Le Mans together for Bentley, winning the LMGTP category both times [2001 and 2002] and we raced together in America too. Like James, he was a complete driver; they were both the complete deal.'

Which drivers were the best teammates?

'Again, James Weaver – he had the smallest trophy cabinet of any of us, because he always ended up in the wrong car. Something always happened to it – wasn't through lack of talent. But he had generosity of spirit.'

Did you find any drivers difficult to work with?

'I probably did, but I'm not willing to name names. Sometimes you'd end up with someone who was difficult to work with, who was not pulling in the same direction as everyone else. In sports car racing, you all have to be on the same page – it's a team sport and you need to get the best out of everything.'

Who do you think was the best of all time and why?

'Ayrton Senna was the obvious one. He was very special. A total nutcase, but a genius behind the wheel. I did one or two Formula Ford races against him, but what I really remember is that in 1982 I had a Formula Ford 1600 Van Diemen, and Ayrton had moved up to FF2000, also with Van Diemen. I was testing at Silverstone, driving round all morning trying to match the GP circuit record, which was 1m 40.1s.

'I couldn't get below 40.3, so I said to Ralph Firman that I thought there may be

something wrong with the car. "I'll get Ayrton to try it," he said, "and see what he thinks." Ayrton had been going round with his FF2000 car with slicks and wings, but jumped into my FF1600 and on his first flying lap did a 40.1, came in and said, "It's absolutely fine." At that point, I realised that I wasn't going to be the best driver in the world, only the second best!'

Who did you have the most fun with?
'When we were racing in IMSA sports cars, there was a whole bunch of us – Corvette's Oliver Gavin, and my Dyson teammates James Weaver, Butch Leitzinger and Elliott Forbes-Robinson. That was our little group; we had good fun.'

Who was the bravest?
'Anyone who could take turn two at Mosport flat. It was a blind downhill left – the place we used to go and watch other drivers. There was so much load on the outside that the shoulder of the right-hand rear tyre used to peel off the rim, and anyone who did that gets my vote.'

Do you have any favourite stories about fellow drivers?
'Mentioning Olly Gavin, I remember when he had a massive accident at Mosport Park in the factory Corvette and was concussed. But Corvette wanted him to tell the TV cameras how strong the Corvette was, and grabbed him while he was still stunned. He was so messed up in his head that like a robot he replied, "My Chevrolet Corvette stood up real well to the accident what I just had."

'He was the complete corporate man when he was racing, and if we were going out for the evening, sometimes we had to get a couple of drinks down him before we could get him out of Corvette World and become Olly again.'

Wallace took a famous victory for Jaguar at Le Mans in 1988, alongside Jan Lammers and Johnny Dumfries. (Motorsport Images)

EMANUELE PIRRO

Interviewed by **PHILIP PORTER**

EMANUELE PIRRO (I)
Born 12 January 1962

Pirro has had a long and varied career in which he's competed at the very top level in touring cars, sports cars and Formula One. After graduating through Formula Three, Formula Two and Formula 3000, he made his Grand Prix debut with Benetton part-way through the 1989 season, as a replacement for Johnny Herbert, and then raced for BMS Scuderia Italia in 1990 and '91. Having raced in touring cars through the mid-1990s, he then became part of the all-conquering Audi sports car team and went on to win the Le Mans 24 Hours five times between 2000 and 2007.

When you were a test driver at McLaren, for your first two years, Senna and Prost were the two team drivers. It would be fascinating to know how they compared.
'This was an eye-opening opportunity for me for many reasons; it really changed my perception and in a way my career. My test team was based in Japan so we only did a few tests together. They were called FOCA tests and [were] in Europe, but of course the contact was continuous, both direct and indirect, and my race engineer was Tim Wright, who was Alain Prost's engineer. The team manager was Jo Ramírez, who was one of the most wonderful people in motorsport and actually one of the few people who really did not have to take one side, because we all know [of] the rivalry between Prost and Senna. Although I don't think they ever really said this to anybody, it was like, "You are either with me or against me."

'So there was a tendency to sympathise [with] or support one or the other. And often, especially about Ayrton Senna, there are stories and interviews and people remember and talk about it. And somehow I feel sorry for Alain. Maybe this would sound rather odd, but he's, I would say, an underestimated racing driver.

'Probably because of the death of Ayrton, there's a lot of sympathy for him. Also because of his ability and charisma and the intensity of the gesture of his driving. He had the ability to share it with people and you could really have a perception that he was giving everything, which by the way, I think is missing a little bit in modern motorsport. Because when you saw Ayrton Senna after the race, you really had the perception that there was no more juice left to squeeze, not a drop, and I think this attracted a lot of sympathy.

'Somehow I can compare it to bicycle racing, which is a very unspectacular sport, but it's a sport with a lot of followers and people really tend to sympathise a lot with the athletes, because you have the perception that they give everything, like a marathon. With Ayrton Senna, he had this ability to show it and so he was attracting a lot of sympathy.

'However, on the contrary, Alain had such a smooth style. But if you see the results, Alain was collecting a lot of fastest race laps so he was an incredibly fast driver, but that was not people's perception. Also, in qualifying, Alain always concentrated on optimising [for] the race. Ayrton was capable of capitalising everything in one lap so people had, in my opinion, the wrong impression that Ayrton was a lot faster than Alain, which I don't think is correct.

'The first year was a pleasure because their rivalry was healthy. It was not unhealthy. Then in 1989, it started to be unhealthy and it wasn't nice. There was more than the rivalry. But, for me, they really helped each other in delivering more than they probably would have been able to if they were alone. I strongly believe that human beings have more resources than we imagine. When you are in a life-threatening situation, you find some extra strength. I think we have a self-protection system that doesn't enable us to deliver everything we have, unless we have some external special motivation. And I think they had this, so they were not really complimentary but helpful to each other.

'The strong rivalry then started to become hate. But when you see the last race of Ayrton, and what he said to Alain, and the way Alain perceived it and told it afterwards, I think hidden, very deep, there was also a lot of respect. Probably afterwards, if he had not died, it would have developed into a special relationship.

'I think this was a very, very special time in motorsport, and a privilege being there. For instance, the way they were analysing the car. We are talking about a new era which looked very modern at the time, but it looks quite old with today's perception, especially when we're talking about the tools that the drivers and engineers had to understand the car, and improve the car in terms of set-up. It was a lot [more] down to the driver's perception and it was fascinating to hear both of them.

'Ayrton especially, I would say, coming from his Dick Bennetts West Surrey Racing Formula Three season, was incredibly analytical, to the extent that he could be

Sparks fly as the Audi R8 of Pirro and Frank Biela heads for victory at Mosport in 2001. (Motorsport Images)

boring, because he would really keep you on a debrief for hours, explaining in the finest detail what the car was doing. So, he would give you every single tool: it's like telemetry, let's say, with a very large number of channels, which could have been somehow confusing for the race engineer. Whereas Alain's debriefs were a lot shorter, a lot more essential. So it was like in today's world, he would only show you the channels that would be really beneficial for the job you had to do.'

Did they share information at all?
'Initially, yes. Later on, less and less. McLaren was very, very good at handling them. I think anywhere else, it would have been an atomic bomb a lot earlier. But Ron Dennis was a very special person with a very strong personality. Jo Ramírez really played an important role in being close to both of them. This is really special because, as I said before, you were either with one or the other one, and Jo was best friends with both.

'So this was an incredible privilege for me to be part of this project. And if I may speak a little bit about myself, it really made me realise that there is a lot more that you can do in driving as fast as possible, and unfortunately, unless you have the privilege to see what the best of the best are doing, you think, "There is nothing more I can do." Of course, when you talk about sheer talent, you could never carbon-copy their talent, but they were doing many things better than me, things that I could learn from them, like attention to detail, focusing, motivating people around them. And so there were a number of things that any racing driver could really get from them. This was really a great privilege for me.'

Turning to sports cars, could we talk about Tom Kristensen?
'[Laughing] I laugh because Tom is a very special animal. He came to the Audi team when we were already established. I joined

in '94; "Dindo" Capello also joined in '94. Frank Biela had been there a couple of years and he was the senior driver in terms of time. We were part of a very beautiful project because at the time Audi Sport was really a privilege to be a part of: there were resources, plans, targets, a lot of special engineering, and special people, and plenty of resources. I wish every racing driver had the privilege to spend a number of years in such a team, where you could really express yourself in the best possible way.

'We started the sports car project in '98 with top-secret status until we made our debut at Le Mans in '99, and Tom came on board in 2000. In '99, there were a number of drivers including Michele Alboreto. So we were Audi Sport. Then this young curly-haired driver joins us and was very welcome.

'We were competitive [in the team] but it was a very healthy competitiveness, mainly because Dr Ullrich treated drivers in an equal way. We had similar abilities so there were no superstars. This contributed to create a very healthy environment, which pushed us to improve more and more, and actually kept us alive in racing terms for many years because the longevity we all had, in terms of racing, has been quite remarkable.

'So Tom joins, and he is a competitive guy. At the beginning, he just wanted to show what he was capable of. He caught us, not really on the back foot, but we were not prepared to have somebody who was so – maybe aggressive is not the right word – but so much wanting to shine. We felt we didn't need to show that one is better than the other: there was room for everybody. We were always pushing to improve the competitiveness, but not to beat our teammates.

'First race in Sebring, for example. This is quite a funny story. So, Tom has been put with Frank Biela and myself with a brand-new R8. The car is very, very good. We do all the testing and then it's time to qualify, and Tom really begs us to [let him] qualify because he wants to do it. One driver goes for the fast lap in qually.

'So I go to turn three, which is the first turn in the complex at Sebring – it's a rather tight left-hander. Sebring has a very bumpy, uneven surface, quite tricky. For qualifying at that time, you go out on new tyres – warm them up, one push lap and that's it, basically. I went there with the golf cart, and Dr Ullrich. We go there and watch qualifying.

'Here he comes, with the screaming sound, coming out of the very fast turn one, which is almost flat for the first push lap, heading towards us, hitting a bump, locking the brakes, crashed right below us, really big crash. When the tyres are just about to get up to temperature but they're not quite there yet, when you lock up you really lose all the grip. There's a big "barrier" of tyres and polyester – it's not like today's standards. So there's a lot of dust. The car is all covered by tyres and polyester blocks and basically we can't see him anymore. So we're worried and we start running because rescue is not like today. I climb over the fence, quicker than Ullrich because of the age difference.

'I dig into all this mess and eventually find Tom's helmet. I hold this hand, and I said, "Tom, are you OK?" I opened the visor and he was absolutely OK but he was shocked, not really so much by the accident but this is not the way you want to start your season. He looks at me and I'm the last person he wanted to see after the crash. But he was wrong because by then Ullrich is the other side of the car. And so I became the second-last person [laughing] he wanted to see!

'Anyway, we won the race and then, of course, Tom's record speaks for itself. We did three years together and it was very good. Frank, Tom and I got on very well. After three years the Audi works operation decided to run one season with Bentley. Some of us were moved to Bentley, which was the same [as] Audi. Tom has been a good team player, a strong driver, a straightforward person.

'I have to say, in those days with Allan [McNish], Tom, "Dindo" and Frank, it was really a pleasure to race because there was a strong rivalry, especially in the short races, but a lot of respect. We used to do some weeks of fitness training in Switzerland and Austria, and always had a lot of fun. Looking back, it was a real privilege.

'We felt Tom was always in the right car for the race. He won more races than us and that's credit to him. Tom was always taking care of his image. We wanted to drive to win races and do our job in the most professional way. But Tom has always been one step ahead in terms of showing the best image he could.'

He was marketing himself?
'Yes, that's correct – marketing himself with more commitment, much more commitment than us, and sometimes we were laughing about it, but he has done very well.'

And how was your relationship with Allan McNish?
'Allan came in [to the team] in 2000, in America, and I knew him very little, but he had had a career already. He drove for Onyx, which was my team in Formula Two and Formula 3000 for three years, so he had a similar path to me.

'In probably the first race that we had together, in America, we were in qualifying and we were in different cars. He was on a push lap, and I was on a slow lap, and somehow I got in his way – 100 per cent accidentally. It doesn't happen very often because normally I took care, but it just happened, so he had to abort the lap. You feel really bad. It was even a close call to crash. So I feel sorry.

'At the end of practice, I go to him to apologise. It's no big deal, not like Monaco Formula One, where if you screw the lap you ruin your chances for the race. And he comes to me in a very, very aggressive way. When he came in [joined the team], he wanted to show well because, of course, it's the nature of a racing driver.

'So he got really upset and I got even more upset because I said, "I come to apologise. If you insult me, if you want a war, here is the war." And so we developed a lot of friction for a long time. But I always had the utmost respect and I felt sorry but, you know, racing drivers, as long as they are racing drivers, you have all the senses and the feelings emphasised. Your reactions are not, let's say, normal. Everything is like salt in the wound. So, a small thing is a big thing.

'I always, always had the utmost respect for Allan but somehow we struggled to talk to each other. Nothing more than this. Until one day, maybe two or three years later, we had to share a car for a long trip from Miami to Sebring, and I realised that he had the same feeling for me – much respect. Since then, we sort of admitted to each other that we were stupid and really respect has always been there. Since then we are, from my side but I'm sure from his side as well, good friends.'

'Dindo' Capello seems to be universally popular among the other drivers.

'"Dindo" is a special guy because he's one of those persons that you cannot dislike. Because sometimes when you interact with somebody, especially another racing driver, there's a little bit of a rivalry. It's something that we have embedded inside of us. We might not like to admit it but there is a little bit of rivalry. With "Dindo", for some reason, he has the ability not to trigger this feeling at all. You just cannot avoid liking him, and he was a strong rival.

'He got in [to the team] from nowhere.

Pirro immediately recognised the competitive streak in Tom Kristensen (left) when he joined Audi. Frank Biela is the man in the middle here. (Motorsport Images)

Basically he had a lot of potential, but very little background. So when he came in, he really was like a junior, although he was not really a junior in age, but in life experience and everything. He didn't want to look smart and experienced so it was easy to laugh with him. Then the way he matured and learned, and grew up, and now, the person he has become, this is really outstanding. Basically almost his whole life experience has been developed with Audi. Really, really a great person.'

How about JJ Lehto?

'You need to find somebody that I don't like! Maybe the friendship is a little bit less because we spent less years together, but we did one season in Formula One.'

He never really succeeded in Formula One, did he?

'It's hard to say because I think the people I mentioned, with the right opportunities, would have done well. And when I say right opportunity, I mean not only sitting in the right car because you do develop. One example can be Damon Hill. His racing path was different. Before he drove a Formula One car, you would not really say that he was a potential World Champion. He got there, being in the right environment, with the right people, with the right attitude.

Which means, "What can I do to improve myself?" not always blaming somebody else when things didn't happen. He had a really incredible season. In today's world, he would have been double World Champion because the accident from Schumacher… In today's motorsport, I think the title would have gone to him.

'What I want to say is that he developed himself into a very, very good racing driver. So I think had he started his Formula One career in a "B" or "C" class Formula One team, he would not have become such a good driver. And so what I want to say is that given the right opportunity means going somewhere where you can really learn, where you can really get everything from people who are better than you, including your teammates.

'I think people like Allan or "Dindo" or Tom or JJ would have done very well. I always believe that some drivers are special so [become] World Champions. Even without the right opportunities, somehow they would have found a way to shine. It's a question of how your career develops and I think JJ was a strong, very strong driver, a very likable person.

'It was a little frustrating in '91 in Scuderia Italia because we were in a very small but good team made up of very, very good people, perfect atmosphere, but very little resources, and a very good car. That year I was still testing the McLaren, and I guarantee [that with our] chassis we had nothing less than the McLaren – we just had a much weaker engine, not because of John Judd not being good, but because of the very little budget that they had to develop it.

'We had the good possibility to shine and JJ took it by putting the car in third place in Imola, where actually I didn't pre-qualify. It's another example of good teamwork. Pre-qualifying was really a trap. We had a good car so, in theory, there was no problem to pre-qualify, but it lasted just one hour, very early in the morning – eight cars, only four go through. We only had to pre-qualify in the first half of the season because afterwards we earned the qualification. Our car was well above that hurdle. But in Imola, he had a mechanical problem so the team asked me if he could use my car. So I did my run, went back very quickly to the pits, gave my car to him and the track is improving at that time in the morning so basically he pushed me out. And having qualified, he finished third. So he's still my good friend, but I was half bitter and half happy when I saw him finishing in the top three.

'But nothing but good memories with JJ. He is a good guy and what you want from a driver is somebody who doesn't screw you, maybe beats you, out of performance, but is somebody you can trust and you can have a healthy relationship with. I was lucky: I had many, many very valuable teammates, from whom I stole a little bit.'

[laughing] **So who didn't you like?**
'In fact, I thought I only had to pick one driver [for this interview]. Somehow I thought it was more down to people who did not quite shine the way they deserved to.

The 1991 Scuderia Italia Dallara was a good car, but the team's lack of budget was the limiting factor. Pirro nonetheless got on well with teammate JJ Lehto. (Motorsport Images)

'So, I had two names for you. One is Mike Thackwell, and the other one is Alain Ferté. Of course they did shine; I don't want to say that they didn't shine, but those were two drivers, I thought, who achieved much less than their ability would have allowed them, for different reasons.

'Mike and I had a strong rivalry, and actually he was my toughest opponent in Formula 3000. He had, and I think he still has, a very odd character, but I always had an incredible amount of respect for him. And I always thought if this guy only had a more normal character, he really would have done a lot of good in motorsport. The reason why I respected him is that he was a very true person, a completely no-bulls**t person, he would tell you what he thought. He thought motorsport was, even then, too safe and drivers were too well paid. He was a racer, period. He probably should have been racing a few decades before.

'The way he was driving both the Formula Two and the Formula 3000 [cars], he was really outstanding. Some drivers out there are being nice with the sponsors, being nice with the media. He did none of these things. I really believe he could have achieved more than he did if he would have dedicated a little bit more effort into what you have to do outside the race car.

'Alain Ferté – a similar thing. He had a lot of speed. We raced in the Formula Three European Championship in 1981. He was the works Martini driver, and he was faster than his two teammates, Philippe Alliot and Jean-Louis Schlesser. He was doing things with a racing car that I never saw anybody else doing. And he was a fun, funny person. He was supported by Marlboro but he did not really give the impression of being a very professional guy because he was a very genuine person. I think Alain was a really wasted talent. If I could rewind and give more opportunities to two people, I would do it for these two.'

In Formula One, in your era, who do you think was the best?

'I would not like to pull a name. It would be easy to say Senna, it would be easy to say Prost, it would be easy to say Piquet… In '92 I was not in Formula One anymore, but I followed all the races for a TV channel. The way I saw Nigel Mansell driving the Williams with the active suspension – I was going along to the tracks and watching. In that year, he was probably delivering a quality of driving that very few people must have achieved in the history of motorsport. So I really think it depends on the situation. I don't like to pick one.

'If Senna had survived, he would have been a very, very good asset for mankind, for humanity. I believe he had a very good heart but he could just not show it because of his competitiveness and because of what he was doing. It's just speculation, but had Senna survived and retired, I would have seen him in a very important role in the world, helping people – a little bit [like] what Lewis Hamilton is trying to do, but I believe Ayrton would have done it in a more structured, professional and effective way. So, maybe it's just dreaming but it's probably a loss for mankind, something for the children. I'm sure he would have done something very special after that.'

Do you have any favourite stories about any of your fellow drivers?

'One! We spoke about so many people but one driver I would like to mention is Roberto Ravaglia. We grew up in karting and initially had a single-seater career, then he went to race touring cars, one year before me. Then I did it as a Plan B, alongside my single-seater career and, together with Gerhard Berger, we were teammates at BMW. Roberto just dedicated his whole career to touring car racing and he won seven championships in a row.

'He was the most complete touring car driver: speed, intelligence, being there at the right time. Most of the championships he won, he won them by a fraction at the last race. I hate to mention luck, so there must be something more than that. And he is one of my best friends.

'I was lucky enough to have a career in an era when you could enjoy yourself a lot without lacking professionalism. Roberto was one of them, and Gerhard Berger and Dieter Quester – guys at BMW. We were laughing so much and had so much fun together. Crazy jokes, but still delivering good performances. And thank God there was no social media! Thank God there were no people ready to judge you on every single thing you did.'

My close friend Murray Walker told me several very funny stories about tricks that Berger played on Senna, which sounded amazing. Did he always have a sense of humour, was he always playing practical jokes on people?

'Yeah! With Senna I think he was at his worst. Sometimes he did something and I would have killed him! [laughing]

'In the touring car days we had Dieter

> **'The way I saw Nigel Mansell driving the Williams with the active suspension, in 1992, he was probably delivering a quality of driving that very few people must have achieved in the history of motorsport.'**

Quester, who was another strong joker. We were racing for Schnitzer, which was the perfect team – very high technical quality but you could really, when the time was right, laugh a lot.

'One time at Donington Park, Dieter came with a [face] mask of an alien which covered his whole head. And so he decided to go out in qualifying on track, without the helmet but with the mask on. With the overlay around the neck, you would really look like a whole green man.

'So he went out and he was black-flagged. He was called in by the stewards. The stewards' room had a glass window and Gerhard, Roberto and I could see him through this window. Dieter was facing us while the stewards had their backs to us. Dieter was trying to apologise and show penitence, and we were showing our bottoms to Dieter so he couldn't stop laughing! Crazy things that added enjoyment to racing…'

PADDY HOPKIRK

Interviewed by **PHILIP PORTER**

PADDY HOPKIRK (GB)
Born 14 April 1933

Paddy Hopkirk became a household name thanks to the huge amount of success he enjoyed in rallying. His first factory drive came with the Standard Motor Company in 1956, and he finished third on that year's Tulip Rally. He then joined the Rootes Group and won the Circuit of Ireland in 1961 and 1962, before making a career-defining move to BMC. In 1964, he won the Monte Carlo Rally at the wheel of a Mini Cooper S – a car with which he would become inextricably linked. He went on to win the Circuit of Ireland twice more in 1965 and '67 – the year in which he also added victory on the Alpine Rally and the Rally Acropolis.

Who, for you, was the very best rally driver?
'Timo [Mäkinen] is probably in my mind the best rally driver ever. He was a very talented driver. And he was a very, very nice guy too, and never up to any dirty tricks. He just was very talented. I'm quite a ladies' man and he had a few girlfriends on the reconnaissance routes. We used to stay in these restaurants or pubs or whatever it was rather longer than we should have because of Timo's affections! But he was a very talented driver.

'One night, we were with Stuart Turner and we were in one of the barges [Austin 1800s], which was one of the service cars with the mechanics, and we had been doing a talk somewhere up around Leeds with Tony Fall, I think. Timo was driving the car, and the mechanics and Stuart Turner were all in it and we were all pissed. He was sober – well, I think he was reasonably sober. It was very snowy and icy on the way back home. He was in the big barge with no studs [studded tyres] or anything on it. I remember sitting beside him and thinking, "My God, this guy has a talent and a feel for a motor car like nobody else has." I always remember that and we got home safely. It was very slippery, but he was in control.

'I've sat with him on a few special stages in Finland when we were practising for different things. He was great. I was very fond of Timo. And he never got up to any dirty tricks. If he knew something that was going to save us all time, a shortcut or something, he would tell us. He was never one for playing his cards close to his chest. Very talented. Lovely man. But he was mad – his powerboat racing... He liked the thrill of going fast and he was a bit mad, yes.'

I thought you were all sane!
'No, no, no, no, we'd all work together but we hated each other when it came to the competition side, really [laughing].'

What do you think made him so quick?
'He was just talented. He had a very good feel for a car. Balance. It's like dancing. He could dance with the car.'

On all surfaces?
'Never really saw him on the asphalt that much. He was much better when the car was not gripping very well. He did a bit of ice racing. All the Scandinavians are just brought up that way. Even when you see Granny in Stockholm driving to the shops, she sort of slides it into the kerb. They're brought up on loose roads.'

And Rauno Aaltonen?
'They called Rauno "the Professor", and I had a sort of a love-hate relationship with him. Rauno was always very secretive, but he was a very talented driver. And he's still going; he's got a school up in Finland with his son. He's very good. I've got to be careful what I say: he was very competitive, though. If he knew something that would help me, he wouldn't necessarily tell me! He would play his cards close to his chest. He used to tell the engineers how to change the steering racks and all that. I think they didn't listen to him that much. He was a very serious driver.

'I remember the first words Timo said to me when I met him in Brighton. Stuart Turner brought him along and said, "This is a new driver who's going to do the RAC Rally, and he's from Finland, and he's called Timo." I said to Timo, "Do you speak English?" and he said, "Yes, whisky, Coca-Cola, please." Those were his first words. Timo liked extremes whereas Rauno was much more serious. But Rauno was a very good driver, and a very competent organiser. His car was very well organised. He thought about the position of the mirror and all that – everything; he would have had notes on it.'

In motor racing, it often helped for drivers to be a good engineer in the 1960s. Was it important for rally drivers to have a good understanding of engineering, do you think?
'Well, I wouldn't have done very well [much laughter]! No, I was quite a good mechanic. I'd had Meccano sets and I rebuilt cars from a very early age, and motorbikes. Yes, I think it does help. Timo was very good, especially with tyres and studs, and

Hopkirk rounds Tabac corner on the Monaco GP circuit on his way to victory in the 1964 Monte Carlo Rally. (BMW)

Hopkirk was quick on circuits as well as stages. This is Le Mans 1964, when he shared a works MGB with Andrew Hedges. (Paddy Hopkirk Collection)

he used to bring Finnish companies to the Competition Department in Abingdon to get the right tyres and what have you. Timo was a great source for that sort of thing, and so was Rauno. Rauno was quite a smart guy, but Timo was a very good mechanic himself. He had very good hands, a mechanic's hands.'

How about Roger Clark?

'Roger was very talented. And Roger's carefree attitude was lovely. He never took himself too seriously, Roger, but he was very good. He was sort of the funny man in the pub the night before, having a few pints, and then going out and doing faster times the next day. So very good, especially in rear-wheel-drive [cars].'

I remember marshalling in Sutton Park on an RAC Rally special section. I suppose it must have been in the late '60s or early '70s, and I was positioned just after quite a tight hairpin through a gate. And it was amazing how many guys didn't get it right. They messed up in some way. He set it up for the corner and came through absolutely beautifully with the tail out and total control. Just perfect.

'Yeah, he was a good sideways man.'

So how about Erik Carlsson?

'Erik had a very unique way of driving – he just went flat-out everywhere. He was driving a car which was built by an aircraft company called Saab and [they were] very, very well built – it didn't break. It had a two-stroke engine and he just kept it flat-out. He was a very tough man.

'I did the Swedish Rally about 100 years ago and I went up to a special stopover in the middle of Sweden. I was with the Standard Motor Company, driving a Standard 10. Erik wasn't in the rally but I met him and he was a test driver for Saab. He arrived in an open Saab sports car and he said, "Would you like me to take you for a run?" and I remember he did and he was very talented and [laughing] scared the hell out of me!

'The car was so underpowered he just kept it going flat-out and he learned how to cope if he went too fast into a corner. He learned how to get around the corner and keep it going and he was a very talented man. He had a great team of mechanics and the reliability of Saab was good. He was a lovely character – he called a spade a shovel.'

He and Stirling Moss's sister Pat were a super couple.

'Yes. They met in Greece while on the Acropolis Rally, I think. We all stayed in a beach hotel which had bungalows out on a lovely piece of land next to the sea, and that's where some relationships were formed! Stirling was one of the first people I met when I came to London from Ireland, and I remember going to the Steering Wheel Club. Stirling was there, and Graham Hill, and I was absolutely starstruck.'

How about Pat as a driver – Pat Moss, as she was?

'Pat was very good. I remember Norman Garrad, who was my team manager when I drove for the Rootes Group. Norman was a very astute team manager and had a very good team of mechanics. He had brought Sheila van Damm into his team. She owned the Windmill Club [which she'd inherited from her father, Vivien] and actually she was a lesbian. I didn't even know what a lesbian was – I'd been brought up as a good Catholic boy in Ireland. Anyway, she was very good for publicity. I think it was [BMC team manager] Marcus Chambers who discovered her. She was very good along with her co-driver, Ann Wisdom, who was the daughter of Tommy – a very influential journalist on a daily newspaper.

'Pat was very competent and a very nice girl. She opened my new shop, my car accessory shop in Belfast. There used to be car accessory shops – you bought your car and then went to a car accessory shop for all the bits you wanted to add on. I have a wonderful shot of her putting on a pair of Paddy Hopkirk driving gloves by the till.'

Do you have any favourite stories about the various drivers?
'Alec Poole is a wonderful guy. He did the London-Sydney [Marathon] with me. I said, "Look, I'm keeping the weight down on this car. I want to see everything [because] we want to carry the minimum weight in this big Austin 1800." I said, "What's that you've got wrapped in a cloth and which you're putting in the passenger door pocket?" He said, "Oh, it's just a revolver." He pulled out this loaded revolver. He said, "It's just in case anybody in Afghanistan tries to stop us or anything." So we actually had a loaded gun in the car. But Alec is a great driver, a great mechanic, and a lovely person with a most wonderful wife.

'Alec is a very good man. I always say about Alec, if the ship is sinking and the skipper says everybody should go forward, and then you see Alec going aft, follow Alec – he is a survivor and is terrific. Being in all the dust and an Austin 1800 for a couple of weeks, you get to know people very well.

'I knew Graham Hill well, too. Graham was a great character. A lot of motor racing drivers can be very boring. With the events we used to go to, such as Sebring and the Targa Florio, there was probably much more camaraderie. Formula One was a very serious business. You're going onto the stage, and you're prepared and you do your job. But I think we actually had much more fun. Graham was very naughty and very funny.

'I flew quite a lot with Graham in his aeroplane up to Scotland, and also we opened the Ulster Motor Show with the Duke of Edinburgh. I met Graham up at Elstree. It was a dirty, wet, winter Monday morning. He gets into the plane and fires it up. It's all damp and cold, a twin-engine thing. He takes off and he looks around and says, "My God, there was a map in here. Where's the map?" He scared the hell out of me. He did break the rules a bit, but we got to Belfast.'

Wonderful.
'When I was President of the BRDC for two years, I tried to change the image of racing drivers. A lot of racing drivers think they're like footballers, and everybody's gonna come up and ask them for their autograph. People don't even know about motor racing, or even that Silverstone exists. When I was there, I tried to get the Institute of Advanced Motorists, of which I'm a Patron, to come in and teach all the rising stars to get them through their Advanced Test. We did that in 2018; the BBC did a piece. It was great.

'I think racing drivers are seen as rich guys who crash cars, have too much money and waste Champagne. And I think that's a bloody awful image, I really do.

'I also tried to get dogs allowed at Silverstone. David Richards did make some jokes about it. They gave me a little dog with a pass at one of the BRDC lunches [laughing]. Hamilton brings his dog to Silverstone and it's lovely. When I went to American circuits, a lot of people had dogs. I said, "We'll get much nicer people at Silverstone if we allow them to bring dogs."'

I remember seeing you with Stuart Turner, who was chairing a panel discussion with Tony Fall, Mike Wood and Roger Clark at the Edgbaston County Cricket ground in Birmingham, in the early '70s. It was a wonderful and very funny evening. You were asked, 'For rallying, what would be the best combination of navigator and vehicle?' and you said, 'Brigitte Bardot and a Dormobile!'
'My God! I just think life's not to be taken too seriously. And so many people do. Graham [Hill] always had great parties when he lived at Mill Hill. For his housewarming, a number of people raced back from Silverstone for a party. He had all the latest music on his gramophone, including the Rolling Stones, and it was such fun.

'I have just one story about Lewis Hamilton. Graham ran this wonderful charity club in north London called the Springfield Boys

Club. I used to go to it and help a bit. One day Jackie [Stewart] brought Lewis up and there were about 150 women there with their children, having done something in Hackney. Kids would be there because of winning something like a running race or football – they would be invited up and Graham Hill, or whoever it was, would hand them the prize. And they would go up with a sort of a coat over their head and hiding [their face] and grab the prize and come down quickly.

'On this occasion, I remember Lewis came and said to them, "For Christ's sake, what are you doing? The image you're giving here to these nice people who have come to present the prizes – don't do that. Turn around, smile at the camera and say hello." You could have heard a penny drop. It was like the Pope speaking and it completely changed. I was very impressed by his command of the situation.'

RAY BELLM

Interviewed by **MARK COLE**

RAY BELLM (GB)
Born 20 May 1950

Bellm enjoyed a long and successful career in sports car racing. In 1985, he started Spice Engineering with Gordon Spice and the team was a front-runner in Group C2 – Bellm won that category's World Championship in 1985, 1986 and 1988. He also took class victory at Le Mans in 1985 and 1988. After a brief foray into Touring Cars, he moved into GT racing and – with Thomas Bscher – helped to convince McLaren to build a competition version of its F1 road car. It was a wise move – Bellm won the 1996 BPR Global GT Series at the wheel of a McLaren F1 GTR.

Of all the drivers you raced against in your career, which ones stood out for you in each decade?
'In the 1980s, it was Hans Stuck – such a brave driver. Without demeaning Derek Bell, he was the power behind that partnership, and had such a great sense of humour. I will always remember Le Mans 1986 and early morning fog; I was cautiously going down the Mulsanne in our C2 Spice, and he came hurtling past me going 100mph faster. I asked him about that later, saying he made me feel like I was standing still. "If you're going to have an accident, you may as well have the accident at 220mph," he replied!

'In the 1990s, it was JJ Lehto; he was so quick in 1995 when he won [at Le Mans]. Then he shared my car in 1996, and I still have the telemetry print-out from that year where he was two seconds a lap quicker than me in the Gulf McLaren. I asked him where I was losing time, and he told me to hit the brakes harder for the first chicane, then come off them. When I tried it, I went straight on! He had an amazing feel for the car. John Nielsen was another very strong sports car driver; he would bully you until he frightened you out of the way!'

Which drivers were the best teammates?
'James Weaver. "Gentleman Jim" was the ultimate sports car driver: he shared all the information with me. He won in everything he drove, and we won the 1996 BPR series together in the [McLaren] F1 GTR.'

Did you find any drivers difficult to work with?
'Gordon Spice could be a nightmare, but he was a very unusual guy. Mike Wilds was mechanically unsympathetic, and I found it difficult to communicate with him. We did some British Thundersports races together in my Waspeze Chevron B36 in 1984, and had a win, but that was it.'

Who do you think was the best of all time and why?
'Clark and Senna. Jim Clark was my boyhood hero, and I have his helmet and goggles from the 1963 Tasman series which he signed. Senna was my grown-up hero when I started racing; he was the best ever. I shall never forget that 1993 European Grand Prix at Donington where he drove around the field in the wet.'

Who did you have the most fun with?
'Gordon Spice, with whom I won all three of my Group C2 titles.'

Who was the bravest?
'Mark Blundell, particularly at Le Mans in 1995. I had crashed our Gulf McLaren during the night in the rain – it just turned round on me without warning, but I was able to get it back to the pits. Then Mark took over and hauled it back up to fourth place.

'That car was horrific to drive in the wet – it was like driving on ice, but he was very brave.'

Do you have any favourite stories about fellow drivers?
'Yes, and they're all about Gordie Spice. His party tricks were legendary – like handstands on chairs with four lit cigarettes in his mouth – and he liked his Captain Morgan rum the night before every race. He always wore an open-faced helmet, because if the safety car ever came out, he would light up a cigarette out on track!'

Bellm was a key influence in the creation of the McLaren F1 GTR. He's pictured (far left) winning at Jarama in 1996. (Motorsport Images)

DAVID HOBBS

Interviewed by **PHILIP PORTER**

DAVID HOBBS (GB)
Born 9 June 1939

Hobbs started racing while he was an apprentice at Daimler/Jaguar, early outings coming in his father's XK 140. He went on to become an outstandingly versatile driver, making his name in sports cars such as the Lola T70 and Ford GT40 during the 1960s, but also proving equally adept in single-seaters – in 1971, he won the US Formula 5000 Championship. Twice a class winner at Le Mans, he was 1983 Trans-Am Champion in a Chevrolet Camaro and raced in series as disparate as Formula Junior and NASCAR. He also forged a successful career as a broadcaster while still racing, and eventually served as an entertaining and insightful motorsport commentator for 41 years.

Who did you have the most fun with?
'That's pretty easy, really – it was Mike Hailwood. He was a fun lad, was Mike. Enjoyed a beverage, as I did. Of course, even in those days, they used to say that drivers shouldn't drink. They did a bit, but now they don't at all. But Mike Hailwood managed to drink a lot and still win 10 motorcycle World Championships and he was always fun to be with.

'It started in South Africa in 1966 when we did the Springbok series. There is a chap called Gordon White, [who was] Lord Hanson's business partner, and he seemed to have plenty of dough. He sent us off to South Africa and we did the Kyalami Nine Hours, then we shot off and did Killarney and Bulawayo and Durban.'

Any repeatable stories?
'We had this mechanic called Bob, who just seemed to make one mistake after another. The first one came at Killarney when I started – it was only a three-hour race so I think we only had one or two stops at the most. I'm leading pretty comfortably, come into the pits and those old GT40s had those great big filler caps just under the A-pillar. Of course we filled with a churn and, having filled it, he then slammed the cap down but he obviously didn't slam it down hard enough. Anyway, Mike got to turn one, which was a sharp left-hander, braked hard – and all the fuel poured out of the filler over the hot disc, right there. The whole thing went up. It wasn't too bad, just a bit of a flash fire but it did singe Mike when he leapt out. So we gave old Bob a bit of a bollocking and complained to Gordon.

'Then we went to the Lourenço Marques circuit in Portuguese Mozambique, where they had a civil war for 20 years, and the race was through the streets. We had jacks that were a very simple device. Well, Bob has one under the front, so the front was up. Then he goes around the back and does the same thing on the back. The only thing about those jacks is they relied on weight to hold them in place. As soon as you lifted the back of the car, it released the weight on the front of the car – should have got somebody to stand on it. So it leapt up and went right through the windscreen. This is race morning!

'Anyway, we ran the race with no windscreen and it rained. And again, I'm driving. I come in for my pit stop and leap out, and there's Mike in the back of the pit in his civilian clothes, reading a book. And he says, "Dear boy, you're doing absolutely wonderfully. It's very dry and warm in here, you can carry on." So I carried on. I think we finished third.

'You always had a laugh with old Mike. Of course, he could play about 10 instruments. He could keep you entertained on the piano, saxophone, guitar... His dancing was amazing, and of course his womanising is legendary. Yeah, we had some good fun.'

Did you find any of the drivers difficult to work with?
'Can't say I did. I had something like 19 co-drivers during my career and they were all incredibly easy to get along with. Paul Hawkins and I drove together and he was dangerously funny to be with. Of course he met a terrible death, the year after he left [the JW Automotive team]. He and I drove in '68 in the GT40s, and then I drove with Mike in '69.

'I drove with Richard Attwood, I drove with Bill Pinkney, I drove with Ronnie Peterson. Ronnie drove with me in the States in the IMSA car [BMW 320i Turbo]. We did races like the Riverside 1,000km, and also the Watkins Glen Six Hours. I set it up; he just drove it. As to set-up, we didn't bugger about like they do today, with half a millimetre ride height and half a pound in the left-front, another quarter of a pound in the right rear, all that stuff. We were more like a couple of pounds up on all tyres. So he was very easy to work with.

'Drove with Hans Stuck a couple of times, drove with Derek [Bell]. I drove with Patrick Depailler, also a lovely guy and very easy to get on with. I drove with Mike Salmon at Le Mans. Michael was very superior: [laughing and imitating his cut-glass accent] "Ah Hobbs, how are you, dear boy? You are looking absolutely splendid today." He used to take the piss out of Ronnie Hoare

Hobbs won his class in the 1962 Le Mans 24 Hours, driving a Lotus Elite alongside Frank Gardner. (Motorsport Images)

[the owner of Maranello Concessionaires] something awful. He was good fun.'

Richard Attwood?

'We were both apprentices at Daimler/Jaguar when we were about 18. He drove my Lotus Elite with me at the Nürburgring in 1962. I'd won the class in 1961 with a driver called Bill Pinkney, who was just a friend. We were very quick around the 'Ring and I went back in '62 with Richard. Richard said, "I'll drive your car and then you can drive my Formula Junior" – I'd never driven a single-seater.

'When I drove Richard's car at Oulton Park, I'm expecting to be a solid fifth or sixth but I won the race easily in his Cooper, which set me on the road to open-wheel racing. He and I were very compatible. Richard was very cautious but we hit it off pretty well, and then the next time I drove with him was in '63 when we drove the Mk6 Lola, the Lola GT for Eric [Broadley].

'We went down to the factory on Monday [before the Le Mans race weekend] and they were running way behind. So Eric said to us, "Why don't you two lads go off to Le Mans and I'll drive the car down on Wednesday, hopefully."

'So we got there and checked into this dreadful hotel and we were hanging around waiting for Eric, and then Eric arrives and there were all sorts of issues with the scrutineers – they couldn't get a luggage box in the back and they didn't like the way the rear-view mirror looked out that very steeply sloped back plastic engine cover. Eric pointed out that there were two side mirrors. "No, no, *Monsieur*, you must have..." So Eric cut a hole in the roof and had a mirror like a periscope.

'We were running quite well [in the race]. Richard's and my lap times were very similar. In those days you couldn't really compare drivers in a race situation because everybody raced at half speed, really, to

103

make sure the thing lasted, unlike now where those cars are so unbelievable – just flat-out from start to finish.

'I had been driving a Lola T70. Got to know Eric very well and also John Surtees. So in 1967 I did Le Mans with Surtees [in the Lola-Aston Martin T70]. He was probably the most picky co-driver, a bit nitpicky. He and Dan Gurney were tarred with the same brush: they couldn't leave the car alone. It would be going well but, "We'll just take a bit more camber out of it, and we'll do a bit of this…"

'I drove on and off with John for quite a long time. And we drove at Le Mans. Well, the thing broke in about six laps. John was driving – obviously he started – and then all hell broke loose between him and Aston Martin. He accused Aston Martin of changing head gaskets, and we burnt a piston. They, in turn, accused John of changing spark-plug manufacturer from Champion to Marchal or whatever, and that's what caused it. There'd been quite a lot of aggro between the two, because the Aston Martin [engine] just didn't have much punch. It really was not what they'd claimed.

'So then we went to Reims together. I never drove at all, apart from a little bit in practice. Driving with John, you never got any practice because he'd just hog the car the whole day, doing the set-up. Eternal, eternal set-up, changing things. We drove at the Nürburgring 1,000km. The right-front wheel came off and got jammed under the fender. Luckily, it didn't roll away.

'At Reims, he got totally fed up with the Aston Martin and we put the Chevrolet engine back in. Anyway, we didn't do any good there, either. Then we went to Brands Hatch, when Mike Spence and Phil Hill were in the Chaparral. We were on pole and they were on the front row. And then it starts to break and, oh my God, in and out… brake issues, and clutch issues, gearbox – everything under the sun went wrong. I finally did a stint but nothing worked – you couldn't select gears. It wouldn't stop, and we just faded away.'

Was he hard on the machinery?
'I don't think so, no. He was very demanding of the machinery and very demanding of his

mechanics. Malcolm Malone, the mechanic, stayed with him forever and was as good as gold really. Then I drove for John in a lot of solo events. Every time something broke. And that was never replicated with Denny Hulme in Sid Taylor's Lola T70. He had Ron Bennett as his mechanic, and Ron was just as cool as a cucumber, and the thing never broke. With ours, something always went wrong because John wanted to experiment with different pitch gears to what everybody else had, different oil, different this, different that to get the edge, and of course he'd have done far better to have just left it alone.

'My best moment of glory with him was when there was a two-part race at Croft. The bloody differential went in practice. We couldn't change it in time for heat one, so the organisers kind of said, "Look, if you only do heat two, you won't get any money because you've got to do both heats." Our team manager was Derek Ongaro, who went to work for the FIA in the end. We'd had such a crappy year, everywhere we went the thing broke. So we did heat two and I started at the back [of the grid] and it rained. We had Firestone tyres and Denny had Goodyear. Anyway, I passed Denny on about lap six, and won by about half a lap. Derek and I were ecstatic, Derek rings John, who nearly had a heart attack — he was going to sue us and sue everybody because we couldn't get any money. We should have just packed it up on a truck and gone home.'

He had a reputation of being a pretty difficult man. Did you find it difficult to get along with him?
'Impossible. But I was a wimp, you know. I thought it was an opportunity for me. I was getting a bit desperate in that I'd been racing for 10 years and nothing much had happened. And I thought if I attach myself to Surtees — who's a World Champion — it's going to be a good way to go. I stayed at his house down in Kent and the dinner-table talk between him and Pat, when he was married to her, was all about Dennis Druitt of Shell.

'They sat there and said, "Well, of course, he gives other people different fuel to us. He gives them better fuel." Talk about conspiracy theories. The whole of life was a conspiracy to thwart John. Everybody was out to thwart John. So he was difficult.

'But then on the other hand, he helped me in some ways. He got me a drive in the Honda Formula One car. He recommended me for that because he realised that I'd had a very sad time with him, and then we went off to Formula 5000, and things were looking very good there. We should have won the Championship twice in America. We kept being late, because he could never get sponsorship. So we missed half the races. First year, we missed exactly half the races — we did seven out of 14 races. I won three of them and lost the Championship by one point. The following year, we missed about four out of 10 and I came third.

'Then I did the unforgivable and jumped ship and drove for Carl Hogan the following year in 1971 and won the Championship easily — won five of the races and won the Championship by miles.'

Can I take you back to Paul Hawkins, who you said was a load of fun?
'I gather that Paul came from a fairly poor background. I don't think he had much money but he was a real "pull yourself up by your bootstraps, get on with it" type of bloke, and made his way to England and started work for Ian Walker as a mechanic/general "gofer".

Hobbs became a familiar face to American audiences thanks to his long broadcasting career. (Motorsport Images)

1967 Brands Hatch 6 Hours – Hobbs and Attwood look on as a seemingly happy Surtees gets into the Lola. (Motorsport Images)

'He and I drove the Gulf car in 1968 and were very compatible on speed and size and everything. Paul and I got on well. The very first race was Daytona, and in those days Bill France was so keen on promoting the 24 Hours and the international aspect of Daytona International Speedway, so there were always two or three cocktail parties. We went to this cocktail party in a very posh hotel in Ormond Beach and the mayor's there and the mayor speaks, and Bill France speaks.

'For some reason, Paul decided that this would be a very good place to have some fun. He had some of those American bangers [fireworks] — Mighty Atom or something — and they made the most horrendous noise. Bloody dangerous things. Anyway he let one of these off in the ballroom, at which point we scuttled out. We went way down south on Daytona Beach and there was a restaurant at the end. We were drinking at the bar and he let another one of these blinking things off. We were chased out of there by some enraged guy — a bit of shrapnel had gone into his leg!

'Of course, next day was the race day and Paul was pretty hungover. But we were actually doing very well in that event and we were leading, but then the fuel tanks sprung a leak.

'Then we were at Sebring; it was as hot as hell. Paul ran into a car being driven by two women — Liane Engeman and Janet Guthrie, who were driving an AMC Javelin and were bog slow. Paul was lapping them and he said she ran into him. In those days, when you were doing those 12- and 24-hour races, you had to drive very carefully, even if you were in a fast car. It was no good just assuming you're going to be all right when you pass people. You had to set it and do it properly. I always think of things like that as being a bit of a 50/50 job.

'Anyway, he went into the press box and said all sorts of what today would be politically incorrect things: [Australian accent] "Bloody women, bloody women should only be allowed in the kitchen..."

'We went to the Glen and Ickx had engine problems so he was a lap behind us. I'm in the pits waiting for Paul to come in to change over. David Yorke says to me, "I say, Hobbs, we want Ickx to win this race so don't push it too hard because we need him to unlap himself." Yorke was showing the "Easy" sign. I'm trying to keep going fast without looking as though I am. Around turn one was Richard Attwood and Paul Hawkins standing right up to the fence, waving me on and saying, "Keep going, keep going!"

'Afterwards, Ickx said to me, "I like to win." I said, "Well, we all like to win but, I mean, do you really call that a win? Not much of a win to me." David Yorke gave me a bollocking for not being a good team member. Next day we met all the Gulf head honchos, including Grady Davis, at the airport and they said, "Hey, we didn't like what happened yesterday at all. We just thought that was pretty low class, blah, blah, blah." And they gave us $1,000 each in cash.

'When we went to Spa, it rained. Oh my God, did it rain. And Ickx, I have to say, showed his true driving ability there. He was something like 45 seconds in the lead after lap one.'

Why do you think Ickx was so quick?
'He obviously had tremendous balance, did old Ickx, as did Mike. I think balance is a very important part of being a race driver because you've got to know "where you're at", as the Americans would say, and all that comes through your backside and ears. Obviously you've got to have good eyesight and assuming you got all those things and your reflexes are good or above average...

'I think Ickx had incredible balance. Mike could sit on a bike, a pushbike, and just sit there with his feet off the ground. Ickx obviously had very big "attachments". He was brave, very brave. Right size – centre of gravity's low. In the wet, he was just amazing. Probably should have been World Champion at some stage.'

How did he and Derek Bell compare?
'I think Ickx was slightly quicker than Derek, but not much. They were a remarkably successful pair and there was quite a big size difference but it seemed to work out all right for them.

'I remember once being with Stefan Johansson when I was competing in the World Sports Car Championship. We were both out and we were talking about what makes people fast. He was driving for McLaren with Prost. He said, "It doesn't matter how fast I go in the damn McLaren, Alain always goes just that bit quicker, or can go quicker more times."

'Over one lap, Gerhard Berger might be almost as quick as Ayrton Senna in a McLaren, but over a 10-lap run Senna is, like, a second and a half in front. Lewis [Hamilton] and Senna were both unbelievably good at overtaking. Chris Amon, for instance, was not. I was not great at overtaking.

'I'll never forget watching Hamilton in the GP2 race at Silverstone – it would have been 2006 and I was calling it [commentating] on American TV. He passed Nelson Piquet Jr and somebody else going through the Maggots/Becketts complex. I mean, it was a thing of beauty to watch.

'Jackie Stewart always used to say [adopting Scottish accent], "Ah well, driving fast, David, it's an art, not just a science. It's not just physics. It's a bit of an art, you know, to drive fast."

'Watching Hamilton pass those guys was really like watching art. It was a fantastic move. And I've seen him do that many times now in Formula One up against people like Kimi Räikkönen. Kimi was driving for Ferrari and Lewis was just starting out in his first year. He outbraked him going through the first chicane at Monza. This is only about his eighth race. And he passes Kimi Räikkönen going down into that, and he made it look so effortless, not messy. He didn't slide into the chicane, all crossed up and out of position. It was just absolutely perfect. These guys, they do have something different.'

What was Mark Donohue like?
'He was very easy to get along with. A bit quirky. He was very Irish and basically very anti-Brit. He always used to say to me, "For a Brit, you're a good bloke".'

What was Vic Elford like, both as a driver and as a character?
'I never drove with him. He was a bit dour, old Vic, I always thought. He didn't have much sense of humour. I can't believe how we've all mellowed and people that you wouldn't speak to before, suddenly, like me and Jacky Ickx, we're all buds. I said to him, "The reason I didn't like you was because I had to let you win. I was only 29 and it pissed me off. Although it was not your decision, you took the brunt of it."

'Now we've all got older, everybody's very mellow. Vic, on the other hand, has got very bitter. I think he's very bitter about how he didn't do better. And he really feels he should have done. I feel that I should have done better, too. That year I was with the [Sunoco] Ferrari [512], we should have won Daytona, Sebring and Watkins Glen – that would have been three nice wins to have on your resumé.

'But as a driver, Vic was obviously extremely good, very versatile. I mean, you win the Monte Carlo Rally in a rally Porsche, and then a week or two weeks later, you win the Daytona 24 Hours. He also won the Targa Florio. He won at Nürburgring four or five times. He was obviously extraordinarily good and probably didn't get the recognition he deserved.

'But then I don't think Brian Redman has ever had anything like the recognition he deserves. Brian Redman won the Spa 1,000km four times. He drove with Siffert. Everyone thought, "Siffert, Formula One". If you talked to John Horsman, virtually everywhere they went Brian always did the fastest lap.

'And Brian had an amazing record. He really did. He won the Formula 5000 Championship three times in a row. The only race he didn't win was Le Mans but he won everywhere else.'

What made him so good, do you think?
'When you talk to him and his wife now, his family life was obviously very tough when he was a kid. His parents sent him off to boarding school when he was six. So I think he was deeply driven. And I think that he had certainly got some of those skills that people like Ickx and Jackie Stewart, Lewis Hamilton and other people have. It's not to say they're all World Champions. I don't think James

Hunt was unbelievably good; I don't think Denny Hulme was, either. I knew I could beat Denny.

'Does that mean I could have been World Champion with different circumstances? Maybe. But I don't think I wanted it enough. I think Brian really wanted it. But he always had a lot of pushback from Marian [his wife], who was terribly conflicted about whether she wanted him to be a driver at all. Every time he got hurt, she said, "Oh, you've got to give up". But of course, he kept pushing on. I think he was obviously very skilful, but he was also very, very brave."

I was going to ask who you thought were the bravest drivers?
'Well, he was definitely one and the other one was Mario [Andretti]. Mario, to me, is also very underrated, I think, on a world scale. You win the Indy 500, which is a lot more difficult than it looks. And you win the Indy Championship, which in those days included racing on dirt, four times. You win the Daytona 500 on your one and only attempt. And you win the World Championship in Formula One. Shows an amazing diversity of talent.

'Again, a little short guy with weight in the right place. And of course, very driven. An immigrant out of a refugee camp in Italy. Mario was very brave. And Brian, in those years when he drove for Carl Haas in Formula 5000, he and Mario duked it out for the Championship three years in a row and Brian beat him every time. To be able to say that you beat Mario multiple times in head-to-head racing, you've got to be pretty damn good.

'I think that Schumacher and Senna obviously were incredibly, incredibly good. But boy, they had a very, very, very dodgy outlook on how you should race, both of them. I've been [commentating on] races in America since 1976, so I've covered a tremendous amount of Formula One races. I don't know how many but it's hundreds. That move that Senna pulled on Prost in Portugal [in 1988] was the first time we ever saw [this type of behaviour]. He ran him right over to the pit wall. I thought, "What the hell is he doing? That's his teammate, apart from anything else." And then they pulled some terrible stunts.

'Schumacher was the same. I think it is dirty driving, quite honestly. Even though I worked with Steve Matchett for 10 years, who was a mechanic on Schumacher's car when he won the World Championship with Benetton, I think that that car probably did have traction control. Yeah, the FIA always said it was disarmed. I did think that Schumacher was a tad better than Damon Hill but that Williams was just the cream of the crop.'

They had such extraordinary ability, they didn't need to break the rules. And they were not playing the game.
'I agree. You've just hit the nail on the head because they didn't need to do that because they were so quick anyway. [Fellow commentator] Bob Varsha and I covered 20 years of Formula One and sports car racing, and in those days we used to go to all the races. You'd stand at the side of the track at Silverstone and watch Senna and Berger when they were driving together at McLaren. Then you'd watch it on the closed-circuit TV in the [commentary] booth. Old Berger would be right out on to the kerb and you'd think, "That looks pretty good". Senna would come round and he'd be just a fraction off the outside kerb and at the end of the lap he'd be like 1.1 seconds quicker – he was just as smooth as silk.

'Schumacher was just the same. Steve Matchett talks about the race in Spain [in 1994] when he got stuck in fifth gear in the Benetton, and he made two fuel stops and still came second.

'A couple of years later at the same race, he drove that bloody awful Ferrari. It rained and he'd gone. In the rain Schumacher was unbelievable. Actually, I was pretty good in the rain because I used to go offline and go around the outside of people. I used to think, "Why aren't they all doing that?" You'd be out there where all the marbles were and all that stuff, which actually, in the rain, would give you a bit of grip with no oil on the track.

Hobbs took a dim view of Senna edging Prost towards the pit wall in the 1988 Portuguese GP. (Motorsport Images)

The other guy who was good in the rain was Jackie Oliver. Brian Redman was good in the rain, too.

'I don't like to think of drivers as being brave. I think of people being brave such as policemen who've got a truncheon and a torch, and they go into the building when they hear somebody in there. That's brave. And soldiers in World War One going over the top. That's brave because you don't want to do it. It's not brave to do something you really want to do, I don't think.

'What we all do have is absolutely supreme confidence in one's own ability. We have massive self-confidence. That was a bit shaken when Jimmy Clark was killed. That really shook me; it shook us all up. We thought, "Oh my God, how can Jimmy Clark get killed? He's just so much better than all of us. It's impossible for him to get killed." And he did.

'That did shake me a bit, but you still always think in the back of your mind, a bit like fighter pilots, I suppose – they had to think, "It ain't going to happen to me." A squadron starts off with 20 guys and in about a week it's down to about four. That's brave.'

Hobbs had a great deal of fun with Mike Hailwood. This is the 1969 Sebring 12 Hours – sadly, they failed to finish. (Motorsport Images)

Did you tend to socialise with the other drivers when you were racing?
'We did. I think we socialised more than they do today. People like Richard Attwood and Brian Redman and I have socialised all our lives, really. Others you got to know. We were acquaintances of Jimmy Clark, because we knew him back in his days when he was going out with Sally Stokes. Sally came from Wolverhampton, so she was very friendly with Richard and Bill Bradley and all the group from MRP [Midland Racing Partnership]. So we did socialise with him and her.

'And then in the days of the Can-Am series, people like Denny Hulme and Bruce McLaren were always very normal and chatty people. Obviously Surtees was hard to socialise with, although we did socialise quite a bit, really, in a way.'

Was there closer camaraderie in those days due to the greater danger?
'Yeah, definitely. Everybody went to everybody else's funeral.'

In your early days, were any of the well-known drivers particularly kind to you with advice or comments or supportive behaviour?
'Funny you should say that. One of the best was Dan Gurney. I drove in the Formula Junior race at the *Daily Express* Silverstone meeting. Denny Hulme and I had the most ferocious dice. Everybody was in that field: Frank Gardner, Mike Spence, Richard Attwood, Peter Arundell, probably Trevor Taylor, Mike Beckwith — and Formula Junior races in those days were pretty frenetic.

'Denny and I just shot away from the field and we were leading by a long way, like 10 or 15 seconds. We had our own private dice at the front. I overtook him a couple of times at Copse. Then, with about four laps to go, the gear lever broke off. I was left with a little tiny stub, about like my thumb. And I used my thumb to push the gear lever forward and my finger to pull it back. Obviously I momentarily lost a bit of momentum when it happened, so there was a bit of a gap between us. And then on the last lap, I broke the lap record and I came second by a whisker.

'Afterwards in the paddock, Dan Gurney was wandering around and he said, "Don't give up. I think you've probably got a bit of a career in front of you. So just keep going. Keep trying. Don't make too many mistakes." I think he probably thought I'd made a mistake in the race; he didn't know about the gear lever. But he was very encouraging towards me.'

Who would you avoid going wheel-to-wheel with?
'Clay Regazzoni. And there was a French guy who had me off at Goodwood. His name escapes me. I never felt very confident around those two. Of course, we all drove in a much safer way because the consequences were potentially disastrous for everybody. You wouldn't lean a wheel on somebody like they do today because, if the wheels hooked up and you went over the top and the car flipped over, you're almost certainly killed.

'Drivers like Michael Schumacher and Ayrton Senna, to me, drove in a highly irresponsible way and, of course, the junior drivers obviously copy their peers and their superiors. Schumacher running Rubens Barrichello nearly into the barrier at Hungary and Senna nearly running Prost into the barrier in Portugal, both races which I was calling on TV, we wouldn't have dreamt of doing that because you could both end up dead. So driving was a lot more gentlemanly.

'People still got stuck in, they didn't hold back. You look at people like Mario Andretti driving on those bullrings of dirt, short paved roads — those guys really got stuck in but they still drove with a modicum of caution. You just did not deliberately run into other people because you knew that the consequences could be disastrous for either one of you or both.

'Senna was the one that set the ball rolling. Quite honestly, for what Senna did to Alain Prost in Japan [in 1990], he should have had his licence hoicked away from him right there and then, and never been able to drive again. Instead of which, in most people's eyes, to millions of fans around the world, he's an absolute hero...'

It went right back to earlier in his career when he was up against Martin Brundle in Formula Three — Martin got ahead of him so he basically took a shortcut and T-boned him.
'At that point, he should have been yanked sharply back, banned for six months or something. Once you start getting away with this stuff, you keep going. I saw him go through most of his Formula One career. Bob Varsha and I went to all the races in those days for ESPN, back in the late '80s, early '90s, and we watched Senna and his skill levels were just uncanny. He didn't need to fall back on all that.

'Stirling Moss, to my mind, was one of the greatest drivers of all time. Stirling undoubtedly also had those uncanny skills. Of course, in those days everybody jumped from car to car — saloon, sports, rallying... He could do everything.'

And he was quicker than Juan Manuel Fangio in sports cars.
'I think Stirling always undersold himself. He always said Fangio was quicker than him in a Formula One car, but I don't think he was. I think that's the difference between today and yesterday. Today, as the junior driver, he would have been pushing Fangio and would have passed him and bugger the consequences. I think Neubauer said, "You can't pass Fangio. He's our team leader and we want him to be World Champion." Stirling also said Fangio let him win at Aintree [in 1955]. I don't think he did; I think he just flat won it. I do think that he was equal to Fangio, for sure.'

I have a theory that Fangio needed to see the front wheels. So he was quick in single-seaters but not so quick in sports cars. And when at the British Grand Prix at Silverstone in 1954, Mercedes-Benz ran the streamliners, he couldn't see the wheels and was hitting the corner marker oil barrels all over the place.
'Exactly. Well, that could be it.'

Who do you think was particularly good at looking after a car and nursing it home?
'We all actually did pretty well at it. Stirling had a terrible reputation as a car-breaker but I think, in actual fact, he was remarkably good at keeping things together. He drove, for example, with that dreadful Colotti 'box, which broke in a frickin' heartbeat. And he tried to be honourable to various people, which probably didn't help him.

'Derek Bell was pretty good at looking after cars, as was Jacky Ickx, because in those days you *had* to look after the car. Nowadays, you don't have to bother about looking after your car. Obviously Phil Hill and Olivier Gendebien were pretty good because those cars broke very easily and yet they still won Le Mans and a lot of 1,000km races.'

MIKA HÄKKINEN

Interviewed by **DAVID TREMAYNE**

MIKA HÄKKINEN (FIN)
Born 28 September 1968

After winning the 1990 British Formula Three Championship, Häkkinen graduated to Formula One the following year with Lotus. In 1993, he became a test driver for McLaren and was promoted to a race seat for the last three races of the season after the departure of Michael Andretti. Häkkinen stayed with McLaren for the rest of his career, surviving a near-fatal crash during practice for the 1995 Australian Grand Prix. He won his first race at the 1997 European Grand Prix and then really hit his stride in 1998 and '99, winning the World Championship in both years. He retired after the 2001 season.

Who were your best teammates?
'I think if this question had been asked when I was racing, I probably would have answered that my best teammates were the ones who were slower than me! But as racing drivers we spend enormous time with our teammates, often when 80 per cent of the time it's s**t. By that I mean all the time constantly fighting with problems, or the rules. Then you look at your teammate in a different aspect.

'I would look at the other side. Where we are out of the car? Are we in a living room, are we back in the factory, are we doing a promotion, are we doing testing, are we in a debriefing with the engineers? So which teammate for me was the person who I enjoyed working with, who is really giving everything for the team and who has a good sense of humour, but at the same time is very serious in all aspects when it comes to that moment of racing?

'I have to say when I was together with David Coulthard for many years with McLaren, it was an incredible time because David had a lot of these great ingredients and these great qualities. He was a great team player, the mechanics loved him, marketing loved him, and he really cared everything for his career. I would say that he was definitely one of the greatest teammates that I had.

'And, of course, I had a little while with Ayrton Senna. I had Johnny Herbert, I had Martin Brundle, Mark Blundell, Nigel Mansell. So I had great guys, but when it comes down to all these ingredients together, I think that David was incredible. When we were going to the racetrack itself, he was very fast. I see incredible qualities, and what he was able to achieve when he was driving a car, when I'm looking back in the history with more time.

'When he was my teammate, I tell you he had some really s****y luck. Winning the World Championship, of course, it's the ultimate. If you fail that, people don't sometimes see the overall picture of what people really achieve, how close they were. The World Championship can't be only one year, and I was the lucky one for winning it in 1998 and '99. David one time had just a crucial moment; he had an engine failure in the Monaco Grand Prix when he was behind me, and I know he would have given me a bloody hard time if he would have managed to finish the race.

'I was wondering all the time, "Is it going to be me or David winning?", which means that he would have been World Champion. But he just had a bad year.'

You had a rather interesting relationship with Johnny Herbert when you were at Lotus. I remember Peter Collins, Jabby Crombac and I following you two in your limousine when we went out to the Tommy Hilfiger factory in Montreal, and all we could see were these two little blond heads in the back of it that kept turning and kissing each other...
'I tell you what, you're right! That guy is a great personality, a great guy. There's no question for it. But the problem with Johnny is, I think the sense of humour of British and Finnish people are based on similarity. Which worked very well with Johnny and me. With all your teammates it's very much a psychological game, and with Johnny I tried to crack a joke sometimes and I would use the Finnish sense of humour, and Johnny was deliberately like, "What the hell is this guy on about?!"

'But he was a very special personality, and the problem was he was so fast on the racetrack it was incredible, and I think that he was a brilliant racing driver. But like I said about David, you need massive ingredients from yourself to match all these elements to be a great team player to achieve the goal. As a personality, Johnny Herbert was absolutely mega-fantastic, no doubt about that. A very funny guy, and definitely one of these guys that if somebody had asked me who I would like to take to Long Bay Island, I would definitely like to take Johnny there, goddammit.'

It's a fairly obvious question, but who did you regard in the early and late '90s as your biggest competition? Presumably it's Michael?
'Yes. I had big challenges to come to Formula One, and when I'm looking at the

young guys today it's a similar thing. It's a big world, it's a big sport, it's a big business, you don't know who your friend is, who is your enemy. It's a tough environment!

'And when I'm looking at that time when I started at Formula One in the early '90s, again there were great drivers out there. I'm talking about Ayrton, who was amazing. An amazing driver. But I felt Ayrton was already a different generation. I felt like my time would come one day, but not yet. I was a little schoolboy coming into Formula One and Ayrton knew already what's happening in this crazy world. Is it politics or is it the teams, how they play the game? Whatever, he knew what it was. So I thought it's better to keep my mouth shut and just learn and listen and look what's happening around me, and my time will come. So I think Ayrton was a tough one.

'And then Michael Schumacher... There's no doubt about it, he was really, really ready for Formula One at a very young age. I felt that in Formula One when he arrived, just after me in 1991, he was physically very ready. Of course, there was no power steering, there was no paddleshift gearchange on most cars. It was a very physical performance to be able to give great lap times in two hours in a race, and I think Michael had that advantage. I'm not saying that I wasn't in a good fitness, but we were at a different starting point when we joined Formula One. Michael, he was definitely dynamite, difficult to beat, and difficult to drive against.'

He must have been one of those guys that you were a bit cautious about going wheel-to-wheel with?
'Oh yeah! He took me off in Macau in 1990; the guy was able to do that. He was a very naughty boy sometimes, and I don't know how the hell he had the courage to do that, because it's like breaking the speed limits on the road. If there's a sign that you are not allowed to cross 70mph and you go 170, I tell you when you look in the mirror and you ask yourself, "Did I do right or wrong?" and then you answer, "No, I didn't do anything wrong," then it's a weird thing. It's a really strange character how you do that, but when you are in the motor racing world and you are on a racetrack, the rules are a bit different when you are racing against somebody. You can play games, you can be a bit naughty. But where you put that line is always very important

2000 Belgian GP, Spa: Häkkinen quietly but firmly explains to Schumacher that he doesn't approve of being chopped at 190mph. (Motorsport Images)

Some drivers seem to expect to win all the time...
'Yeah, it's a bit freaky, but in Formula One either you lose or you win, and Michael's attitude was, "I just want to win all the time; I don't want to lose." And that makes a difference for me, because if I lost a race I was super pissed off, of course, but it wasn't for me the thing that would change the world, because we are here for a long time. Well, hopefully for a long time. And this one Sunday, it's not going to change anything in our life.'

Tell us about your fight at Spa in 2000, how Michael chopped you early in the race but you caught up and made that superb pass approaching Les Combes...
'That race was such an incredible feeling. I was so fast in the McLaren, but after that incident I had to catch up. It was frustrating for me for a time because I was so fast, and he was so slow on that straight after Eau Rouge. It was beautiful to follow him and to catch him. I was like 10kph quicker than him, like I had DRS! I was so quick it should have been so easy to overtake him. But that was the only place where I was so much quicker, and Michael was able to close the door there all the time – when we were doing over 300kph [186mph]...

'I was thinking about the laps getting less and less, and if he continues like that, this is not looking good. Then luckily Ricardo Zonta was there and that was my great opportunity. As soon as I saw Michael go to Zonta's left, I went to his right. He told people later he never knew I was there, so it was a good job he didn't move! It was such a great "up yours!" moment after what Michael had done earlier. Absolutely, no doubt about it.

'It was a brilliant moment, and I think these kind of manoeuvres and overtakes become history. That's why I like to remain an ambassador and part of McLaren these days. It's great to talk to people there; the young guys and young girls remember those things. For me it's like yesterday and for them it's like such a strong childhood memory, which brought them to be a fan of Formula One. So it's interesting to see these young team members and fans, how they see the past.'

Who do you reckon is the bravest driver you ever saw?
'That's interesting because being the bravest works in different ways. To do a stupid manoeuvre, I don't call that to be brave. There were a lot of drivers who did some incredible overtaking manoeuvres fighting for their position, which didn't make any sense whatsoever, and I don't call that brave. I call that stupid and a lot of drivers when they were racing out there in my career, they would drive in such a way that they weren't thinking clearly what they were doing.

'But when we are talking about who were the most really brave drivers out there, I think in a clever way it was Michael and Ayrton, or Ayrton and Michael [in that order]. I had a couple of manoeuvres where I really had to stop thinking about what might happen. Where I was thinking that's the way it's going to work out, I know what I'm doing, rather than thinking about if it doesn't work out, it's going to be a big one. Those two were able to do things like that a lot of times; it was weird!'

Do you have a driver that you think of as the best of all time?
'Well, if I look at what Lewis has done in his career, it is incredible. He has been able to keep his mind and body in a good shape. That is the biggest challenge. There have been great drivers in the past, at certain periods of time, but Lewis has been able to keep this form such a long time and that, for me, is an incredible achievement.

'I am looking differently also at today's physical technology. How Hintsa Performance, for example, can advise and develop the drivers to maintain their performance during a season, in the off-season, and then the next season, psychologically and physically. This area has developed so hard that, like with athletics, they can go on for years. In my time this wasn't so developed. So your sporting career was much shorter.'

Did you have any favourite circuits?
'I have many favourite circuits! I've had some circuits where I've had some great results. In Barcelona I had a great result. But when you're really, really looking forward to going to a racetrack and you're looking forward to going through the corners and experiencing the g-force, I have to say it is Spa. That was an unbelievable track to drive. You really felt the power of a Formula One car in terms of

'As soon as I saw Michael go to Zonta's left, I went to his right. It was such a great "up yours!" moment after what Michael had done earlier.'

that g-force, the acceleration and the loads that the suspension has to take. Spa was definitely the place.

'Monaco is where you put everything on the limit: the car, yourself. So it was beautiful to experience that, too, but Monaco is something that when you are going to that track you don't really look forward to it because you know that the risk of going off there is so high, so that's not so much fun. But Spa... it was amazing!'

Let's talk about Adelaide 1995. How hard was it for you to come back from that accident, and did you think you could still be quick when you first got back into a car during a test at Paul Ricard early in 1996?

'I think the biggest advantage in that situation is that I was young and very, very fit. I tell you what, though, in the time when you are in the hospital and in that poor condition, you just don't want to have even the slightest thought about racing. You don't want to think about it because you are in such a catastrophic situation. You don't know if you are going to recover and become a normal person anymore. And then when you are first able to go outside the hospital, you are walking like an old man, slowly and having such pain all the time. You are thinking, "Hell, when am I going to get back home? What am I going to do?" and the pain is just taking all your energy and all your thinking.

'So the time after finally landing in Nice Airport and coming back home to Monaco, I was still destroyed, and sitting on the terrace watching the evening sun going down thinking, "What the hell is going on here? What am I going to do? What do I want to do?"

'And the clock was ticking, and I knew that they would come and would ask me, "Mika, now you have to make a decision otherwise we have to find another driver." And when my first test finally came in front of me it was quite a scary moment, but not because I wasn't fully aware of my condition. I was slowly coming back to normal, but I was worried about the impression of the mechanics, what they would think. I wasn't the same anymore because part of my face was paralysed. They had shaved my beautiful blond hair! I was thinking, "I look like a damn monster, coming here."

'I was really a bit worried, and I thought, "OK Mika, just let it go. Go and sit in the car and see how you feel." And I felt great. I wasn't scared, I felt strong, and I wanted to prove to the team that I wanted to come back and it just worked well. I didn't allow

Häkkinen negotiates the corner where he would later crash so disastrously during practice for the 1995 Australian GP following a tyre failure. (Motorsport Images)

myself to be sick. I didn't allow myself to let people think I was in a bad condition. I was fast, and all the time fighting that way. "I'm OK, let's go back in and let's talk about racing. Let's not talk about Mika, let's talk about action. You don't have to talk about my accident anymore. It's history. Let's move forward."

'It was quite a difficult moment, because you don't give yourself that time to think about what's really happened. Of course, I had the time after my accident, but it was different because I was in pain. But thinking about it now, it was the right thing to do. You have to go back, if there's nothing physically stopping you. You have to go back and continue to kick some ass. And that's what happened.

'The biggest thanks go to the team, all the friends who helped me in Australia and, of course, my family, my ex-girlfriend, my ex-wife. There were a number of people who just gave me huge room to recover, and it was an experience which I will remember for the rest of my life.

'Now I can say to my kids, "Take care of your friends, take care of your business partners. Look after them because one day you may need the people that aren't working just because of the money but because they like you, your character."'

RICHARD ATTWOOD

Interviewed by **PHILIP PORTER**

RICHARD ATTWOOD (GB)
Born 4 April 1940

Although Attwood raced for the likes of BRM, Cooper and Lotus in Formula One – and finished second at the 1968 Monaco GP – he is best remembered for his successful career in sports cars. Through the mid-1960s, he was often to be found sharing a Ferrari with David Piper, and then in 1969 he signed for the works Porsche team. He was part of the team that developed the initially wayward Porsche 917, and in 1970 Attwood and Hans Herrmann mastered dreadful weather conditions to win the Le Mans 24 Hours in a 917K. The following year he won the Österreichring 1,000km with Pedro Rodríguez in a Gulf-JW Automotive 917, before retiring at the end of the season.

Attwood leads BRM teammate Pedro Rodríguez at Monaco in 1968. The British ace finished second. (Motorsport Images)

Who were the teammates with whom you most enjoyed working?
'I suppose the ones you got on well with would be the ones who also did a similar performance to you. So as a team, you worked, not against each other but more with each other. But the guy who was always perfect in that direction was Lucien Bianchi.

'He really wanted to be English, rather than Belgian or French, I think [laughs]! He was just a lovely guy. And he always brought the car back. He was consistent. We got on really well. I drove with David Piper a lot, too.'

What do you think made Jacky Ickx so good?
'Oh, God! You find the fastest drivers always get good cars, don't you? I think the way you settle into a team helps a lot.

'In 1968 I drove the [Ford] F3L, the 3-litre prototype that Alan Mann ran. It had that fantastic [Cosworth DFV] engine. I drove it twice only. The car never finished a race so they never did any good with it. I liked the car because in most races it did, it was either on pole or did the quickest race lap. I raced it at the Nürburgring with Frank Gardner, and Frank did the Martini Trophy at Silverstone and he also drove it at Spa, where he was on pole with that car. Frank was not the bravest driver, but he was seconds ahead of me in the GT40 – that's how fast it was. If you can just get yourself into the fastest car, it breeds confidence. It's just a mental thing.'

Talking of the mental side, did drivers have particular favourite circuits? Did they go better at some than others?
'Well, they did, but you have days or the car that happens to suit the circuit. And that circuit then can become quite good for you. There are lots of stories about Spa, which everybody dreaded because it was so bloody dangerous.'

You raced against some amazing names.
'Jim Clark was the stand-out. He was just different. He had a sensitivity that was uncanny. The H16 BRM was a disaster, just like the V16. And yet Clark managed to win a race with that engine. Nobody else did. He was just amazing. He just had senses that other people don't have – he was so soft and smooth. There was nobody like him. The 1½-litre formula was just right for him.'

In contrast to Graham Hill – it's always said he had to work very hard at it.
'Clark was the born natural and Graham was the complete opposite. He started so late in life. Most mechanics end up shunting the cars but he grabbed his chance with both hands and found he was quite good at it. From thereon, he worked so hard at it.

'He used to get the car by the scruff of the neck – bit like Nigel [Mansell], I guess. Clark was so smooth – he would go through all the gears to brake for a corner. Graham – forget all that. He was going to brake like fury, not using the engine to brake at all, and just slot it into the gear he wanted at the last second – from, say, sixth to second, if you like. He thought he could brake quicker that way. I'm not saying he couldn't, but his methods were totally different and he would literally throw a car, not caress a car, he would urge it into the corner and hoof it.

'I drove one or two of his cars, testing or whatever. They had a very short throttle pedal. With Graham, the throttle was either on or off – as simple as that. Clark's would have been much longer with more feel. So the styles were completely different, and yet they were such competitors together.

'We were out at the Tasman series one year. We went out for dinner one night and the hotelier was very proud of his cellar. He produced a bottle of wine and Graham tried it. The weather was very hot, all the windows were open and we were on the ground floor.

Graham tried it and, just to get a reaction from us all, he said, "Oh, that's absolute piss." With that, he got the bottle and threw it out the window! This might have been a hugely expensive bottle of wine, I don't know. The proprietor was obviously very upset about this and he thought, "I've got to appease this chap." So he brought another out.

'Well, of course he brought three or four out and the same thing happened to every bloody bottle! It got to the point where you just couldn't help but fall about laughing. He knew how to do it – his timing was just

legendary. He was really a born, unpaid entertainer. He loved doing it and loved being the centre of attraction. We all loved him doing it and were egging him on to do more.'

How about Jackie Stewart?
'Jackie learnt everything from Jim Clark. They went around together a lot. Jackie modelled himself on Jim Clark, even the way he walked. I think Jackie had the skill set as well, because he did it in shooting – a quick eye and reactions and God knows whatever else that falls in line perfectly with racing. But I would definitely say that Jackie had to try a lot harder than Jimmy to get to where he got.'

What about Jack Brabham?
'Jack was all for Jack! He was a great innovator and he knew where he was going pretty much all the way along. To make his own car was definitely on the hit list. He was quite an engineer as well. He saw how Coopers were made and he thought, "Well, I can do that."

'Whenever he overtook you, which he did quite a few times to me, he used to – and it didn't matter who it was – he used to shower them with s**t. He'd go off-road to do that. One often would hope that he'd actually get a puncture by doing that, but he never did! It was a most extraordinary characteristic which I think, in a way, was disrespectful, but he didn't give a s**t.

'I find that extraordinary. He was the only driver that did that. I suppose he was trying to rub your nose in it. I don't quite understand that story, but everybody says he did it. Maybe he didn't do it to Jim, I don't know.'

He did it to Stirling.
'I find that disrespectful, being a bit serious, and it could do damage. I followed a car once, and it was totally unintentional, but a stone was thrown up that was on the track, and went through my goggles. So when you know that sort of thing could happen, why would you?'

How about Dan Gurney?
'I didn't come across Dan, really. I had great admiration for him in his Eagle when he finished at Reims and he got his first championship point [in 1966], so I went to congratulate him. Dan was a grandmaster: he had everything, he had good looks, he had a tall frame. That meant he was heavier than most other guys and he had to make a special car for himself.

'He was a very clever guy. I only read the other day about his Le Mans win with Foyt. He worked out before the race that the car he'd got was fast enough. He said, "We're just going to let these other young chargers bugger off if they want." They qualified ninth. He was asked what was wrong with the car. There was nothing wrong with the car [laughs]. They couldn't understand why he wasn't on pole. You don't have to be on pole for Le Mans.

'He was just a very clever guy and ingenious. He made his own car, with limited resources, I'm sure, and even his own engine. Just an amazing guy. Massive respect. I loved him. He was so nice with it, and Jim Clark was exactly the same type of person. Jim almost didn't know how good he was, it was like a mystery to him.'

JODY SCHECKTER

Interviewed by **PHILIP PORTER**

> **JODY SCHECKTER (SA)**
> Born 29 January 1950
>
> Scheckter made his Formula One debut in 1972 and in his early days had a reputation for being fast but wild. After joining Tyrrell in 1974, he matured into a consistent, intelligent driver, and won his first Grand Prix that year in Sweden. He moved to the new Wolf team for 1977 and sensationally won its debut race in Argentina, and was second in that year's World Championship. Two years later, Scheckter won the title for Ferrari after seeing off the spirited challenge of his teammate Gilles Villeneuve – fittingly, he was crowned on the Scuderia's home turf at the Italian GP. He retired at the end of the 1980 season.

Can I start by asking how you rated Niki Lauda?

'He's probably the top of the list. I had a lot of respect for him, probably more than any other driver. He only bulls***ted me once – when he said he wasn't going to come back, and then he came back the next year [laughing]. There's some drivers that you can drive next to in any type of situation and you know that you'll feel good about it, there won't be a problem. He was solid, a very solid guy and I had a lot of respect for him and I think he had respect for me.'

How about James Hunt?

'Ah, James. I got friendly with James because we lived in Spain, next to each other. How do I sum up James? I think he had a very good one-and-a-half years, maybe a little bit longer than that. I think some of his habits, probably, were his downfall. I remember picking him up from Watkins Glen because I had to take him to the airport at six o'clock in the morning or something. And I don't think he had had a bath or anything since he had got out of the car. He smelled like mad, I opened the window and had to drive like that [indicates hanging head out]. In a sport like that, it'll just get at you.

'I remember once at the Nürburgring, "Let's go for dinner afterwards". After a race, I've got to just wash and have dinner [but] I think it was like nine o'clock and we hadn't eaten yet. So that was his problem. I think it's just sad, very sad at the end. He was a lovely guy and all that, good at tennis and stuff like that. I went to America and wasn't close when he was doing all of his work [as a commentator with the BBC], and there was a clip of him trying to get into a club, and the security guy and him had a fight, which was very sad to see. But yes, nice, nice guy.'

Pretty good driver?

'Oh yeah, I think for a period of time. I remember another incident: at Paul Ricard [he] was trying to overtake me. The corner into the straight – one time I'd go slow, one fast, and put him off. I remember at the end of the race he came and said, "I learned something from you."

'The other thing I remember is that he was going for the Championship [in 1976]. At Watkins Glen, he came up [behind me] and I didn't give him a hard time. I could have kept him behind me but I always have respect for somebody that's going for the Championship and I'm not. It was not that I didn't race him but I wouldn't push as hard as I could to keep him behind me.

'We lived near each other and we went to some parties together. He was a great guy.'

How about Gilles Villeneuve?

'As you know, Gilles was my teammate [at Ferrari]. We were very close. I suppose I pride myself in knowing that I never had an argument or even a bad set of words with any of my teammates. Gilles was a very honest guy – very, very naive, I think. He worked very hard at his racing. He loved the image of being this wild maniac guy. For me, that was his weakness and actually gave me some confidence when we were going for the Championship, because he had won a couple of races and I was number-one driver in writing. So that put a lot of pressure on me.

'He could have won the Championship, no question about it, but he made some mistakes, and I think he did things which were helping the car to be unreliable. You don't win Championships like that. I think I'd been around long enough to know that to win Championships, you've got to finish. Even if you don't finish a little bit ahead, you've got to get points.

'Very honest, but naive guy. We were very friendly together. And he was a good driver, no question about that. But the wildness and everything was more of an act – I'm not saying he wasn't wild, but a lot of it was an act. I went to Modena [by road] with him and I said, "You're going to drive slowly now. You're not going to do stupid things with me in the car." He was fine until we got like a kilometre away from the [Ferrari] factory and then he started skidding and all of that.

'It was the same thing when I went up in a helicopter with him. It was the time when he'd had the argument with Pironi [at Imola in 1982]. I was retired at that time. The team

Scheckter leads Villeneuve at Monaco during his title-winning 1979 season. (Motorsport Images)

didn't back him. We had a rule when we drove, and if you were one and two, or three and four, you did not fight. Pironi didn't abide by that, and the team didn't acknowledge that and he was very hurt by that.

'Gilles and I were very honest with each other, because that's the only way you can stay a good teammate. You find something that's a little bit better [on the car] and he'd say, "What do you think?" You feel like saying, "Oh no, it wasn't very good at all", but once you start doing that it's just a deterioration of a relationship.

'Anyway, I went up to Italy with him in a helicopter, fine, until we got near, and then he was starting to do his little tricks. But I liked him a lot.'

What about Alan Jones?

'Alan Jones… I remember being in Brazil, and he said, "Let's go out together." So we're going into this sleazy place and I'm thinking, "God, I shouldn't be seen here." And I walk in and the one girl says, "Hello, Alan." Obviously he was a regular customer in that place!

'He was only a good driver; he had a great car. You know, the Williams at that time was by far the best car. I would say [he] was very selfish, but I suppose a lot of drivers were selfish at that time. I remember at Monza when I was going for the Championship, I said to him, "Let's not fight too much. I'm going for the Championship." I knew it wouldn't mean anything to him. I wasn't great friends with him.'

What are your memories of François Cevert?

'Well, it's difficult for me because I didn't really know him very much. I'd had a crash with him in Canada [in 1973] – I only did a few races for McLaren that year but I was going to be his teammate [the following season at Tyrrell]. At the next race I think we

Scheckter forged a close relationship with Gilles Villeneuve while they were at Ferrari together. (Motorsport Images)

had some words and said, "OK, put it behind us." And then he was killed at that race, at Watkins Glen.

'I was the first person on the scene. I jumped out. All I remember is that the spark plug was shorting. I went to try and get him out, and I don't remember what I saw, but I turned around and walked away. Somebody sent me a picture, some years ago, with me with my hands up, signalling to the other drivers that it was over. Thank goodness I didn't see what had happened, but that's the only experience I had with François.'

How about Mario Andretti?

'Well, if you know how he won the World Championship… [Pause] He had it written in the contract, and they abided by it, that Ronnie could not beat him. I remember Ronnie saying to me that they put him out on full tanks in qualifying, and did all sorts of things like that so Mario was faster. Mario admits that, if you look at the [programme] on Netflix. I watched that and he admits that was the deal. Ronnie could not overtake Mario.

'You know, there were some drivers that didn't support safety. I lost respect for them, and they just were selfish in their own little way: "I'm not going to do anything. I'm just here, I'm just gonna do my thing and go," and he was one of them. Alan Jones was another. Keke Rosberg was another. Ickx was another one that would just not listen. "I'm doing my deal. I'm getting in and out." I felt that was very selfish because drivers were getting killed each year.

'The next thing I remember [about Mario] was at a go-kart race in Paris. I wasn't a go-kart driver. I went to one practice in England and then went out there. Anyway, I caught him up twice and went over the back of him, because he made me slow down too much. I thought I was going to get the Mafia after me! He complained that his engine wasn't fast enough, but some of the American drivers have a different attitude.

'I remember [once] letting him get a tow from me in practice or qualifying. I was so far back on the grid, it didn't make any difference to me what he did, and he thought that was very strange that somebody would do that. I'm not going to do anything negative to somebody if it's not affecting me.'

How did you find Carlos Reutemann?

'[Laughs] Carlos – I didn't really know him from a driving point of view, but he was a guy that was so suspicious of everything. I always remember him going and looking at the tyres and what number have you got and is it the same rubber? I think you could get to him very easily with all that sort of stuff.

'I was going to be his teammate, because he was driving for Ferrari. Ferrari came to me and I signed up at the beginning of '78 [for 1979]. I signed up as number-one driver and he was driving for them. So I said, "Can we meet somewhere, just to discuss [things]," and he wouldn't meet at his place, he wouldn't meet at my place. We had to meet in the middle. This was in the south of France. So we met in the car and I said, "Listen, we're going to be teammates and we need to get on," and all of that – and then he left [the team]. He obviously got some good results, so he was a good driver.'

First race for Tyrrell – the 1974 Argentine Grand Prix. Sadly, Scheckter retired. (Motorsport Images)

How about Nelson Piquet?

'When I was sort of getting ready to go out [retire], he was coming in. I remember in

Having won on home turf in South Africa in 1975, Scheckter (left) celebrates with teammate Depailler. (Motorsport Images)

Canada, it was one of his first races, and he held me up – young upstart! He did things differently. His results show what he did: obviously was very good and a very smart driver.'

Another Brazilian, Emerson Fittipaldi?
'One of the top guys for me. I would say him and Niki are the guys that I put in the top bracket. Lovely guy, and I think he was a very good driver, too. Nice, really nice guy – I went to his house in Brazil. Yeah, one of the lovely guys in motor racing, and very, very quick.'

How about another Brazilian from that era, Carlos Pace?
'I don't remember much about him except Argentina [in 1977]. I was in my first race in the Wolf, and we weren't that fast, but it was hot, hot, hot. I came through the field and I came up behind him and he was taking all sorts of funny lines. Then I passed him and I won the race. He had got sick in his helmet, that's how overheated he was.'

What are your memories of Alain Prost?
'Alain was just coming in, when I was sort of going out. I was the head of the GPDA, which is [the body for] the drivers talking about safety, and as a young driver he was very strong on his ideas. I saw him as a very good driver. And I said to Mr Ferrari, "You must hire him." When I was leaving, I said he's the guy that you need to hire. He didn't, and he hired Pironi. Prost and Lauda were very good at setting up their cars.

'I had a weakness and a strength in that I could drive around any problem. So that meant I got to the race with all the problems and I drove around them the whole time, whereas those guys, I think they adjusted their cars better than I did. So they had an easier time and a better car in the race, and it shows in their results.'

How about in the wet? Who would you say was the best or particularly good in the wet?
'I think I was one of the top guys in the wet. I know that Gilles was. There was a race when Gilles was much faster than me, but most of the time I was as good as anybody in the wet. In South Africa [in 1979] I put on dries, everybody else was on wets. I was second for about four laps with dries on and the only person who pulled ahead was Gilles. I should have won that race but the tyres collapsed.

'In Belgium [in 1977] I was 10 seconds ahead in the wet and it started drying. I thought, "I'm just going to take a little bit more road and touch the kerbing." I touched the kerb, spun and I was out of the race. But I think in the wet I was probably as good as anybody.'

Why do you think you were so good in the wet?
'I think it's probably more riding around problems and car control. At Brands Hatch they had a race very early on, in March I think it was [the 1976 Race of Champions]. It was very cold. The tyres were hard; you couldn't get them to warm up. I think I was on pole by about a second and a half or something – only because I could slide the car so much that the tyres would heat up, and I would be fast. But I crashed on the first lap, so I wasn't so smart!'

Is there anyone you would have avoided going wheel-to-wheel with?
'Yes! Jarier. There's some drivers you know are going to be dangerous; some drivers you know are going to be safe. And there's Jarier. He took me to Watkins Glen one time, from the hotel to the track. I think we nearly crashed three times going to the track. Yeah, he was one of those drivers that you could never understand what he was going to do.'

I always remember James Hunt, when he was doing the television commentary with Murray Walker, saying, 'Well, that's just the sort of pig ignorance you'd expect from Jarier'!
'[Laughs] I suppose Alain Prost was really the first very, very good French driver that I came across.'

Did you find any other drivers difficult to work with, or any who would play psychological games?
'No, not really. I always worried about myself and not about other people. So, I didn't think, "Oh I wonder what he's doing or they're doing." I just worried about myself and I think that was the right thing to do.'

Who did you have the most fun with?
'Probably James and Gilles. And Patrick Depailler was my teammate for three years. A lovely guy. He had a bit of a loose head. He was arrested going to a circuit – I think it was Dijon – because he was late and he overtook all the cars. Ken [Tyrrell] had to go and get him out of jail for the race. When I was racing for Ken in Argentina, Patrick was having a sip of wine at lunchtime, which I couldn't understand. But we had a great relationship.

'I used to say, "How are you going around that corner?" He said, "Ah, quite flat, quite flat." And I thought, "F*****g hell." When you're young, you think, "I'm going to do it like that and I gotta just hold on. If he's doing it flat, I'm doing it flat."

'About three-quarters of the way through the season, I discovered that, "Quite flat" meant "Not quite flat"!

'Lovely guy, nice teammate. He went quickly, I think, and as time went on he went quicker. I didn't like the concept of the six-wheeler but he did and so they started listening to him more. I'd say typical French. We went testing and on the first day, we were quite quick and he said, "The car eez beautiful, it eez fantastique." The next day, other guys were faster than us, whereas we were doing the same times [as the day before]. "Eeet's s**t."

'Jabouille was a lovely guy; I enjoyed being with Lafitte. I was very friendly with the French drivers. And they were the only drivers that really seemed to stick together, be friendly with each other.'

How about Clay Regazzoni?
'I was at Dijon, I think it was. I was trying to qualify and he came out of the pits and came straight in front of me, and just messed up my lap. So I went in front of him and made him stop. I was about to get out of my car and punch him in the face but I didn't. I think I cooled down or whatever.'

Jody, thank you.
'I've probably made some more enemies!'

JOHN FITZPATRICK

Interviewed by **PHILIP PORTER**

JOHN FITZPATRICK (GB)
Born 9 June 1943

John Fitzpatrick first made his name in the British Saloon Car Championship, and in 1966 he won the title outright in a Broadspeed Ford Anglia. As the 1970s progressed, he moved into the European Touring Car Championship with Ford and then BMW, and became increasingly involved with endurance racing – he went on to win his class at Le Mans three times. After moving to the US to join Dick Barbour's team for 1980, 'Fitz' won the Sebring 12 Hours and a host of other races, before deciding to start his own team in 1981. John Fitzpatrick Racing ran Porsches for the next six years, and in 1983 'Fitz' and Derek Warwick took their 956 to victory in the Brands Hatch 1,000km – humbling the works cars in the process.

Which of the many drivers you drove with would you say were your best teammates?

'That's a really difficult one because I was lucky to have some really good teammates. If I was to pick the absolute fastest, it would be difficult because they were all incredibly good, but I would say probably it'd be a close one between Derek Warwick and Thierry Boutsen.

'Thierry was, in my opinion, a very underrated driver. He never got into the best car at the best time, or the right car at the right time. But whenever he drove in 956/962 Porsches, he was always top of the list. He was fantastic. I suppose the 956 was as close to a Formula One car as you could get. And you would never meet a nicer guy. Very unassuming, very quiet, not pushy – but as soon as he got into the car, whoosh, he was away!'

That's very interesting and different. What do you think made him and Derek Warwick so good?

'What does make a racing driver good? I suppose concentration, determination, feel...? You have just got it, or you haven't got it. I co-drove with Derek and Thierry a lot and they were always just that bit quicker than me. I used to think, "Why the hell are they quicker?" and I used to talk to them about it. But they were just quicker. Whether they had bigger balls, I don't know [laughing]! Most guys I drove with, I was equal to, a match for, but those two were outstanding.'

Who did you have the most fun with?

'Well, I had a lot of fun with everybody. I mean, Hobbo [David Hobbs] is very funny. Hobbo is a very, very amusing guy, very dry sense of humour. We had a lot of fun; really enjoyed having him in the car. I took it seriously in one way, but in another way I was out there to enjoy myself because I made a living out of it for a while. I knew I wasn't good enough to be a Formula One World Champion. I just did the best with what I'd got. I was out there to really enjoy it. That doesn't mean to say we didn't try hard. We did want to win, of course we did, but perhaps I would have had a slightly different attitude if I'd been doing Formula One.

'I was lucky in having some really good drivers and super-nice guys to drive with us. Derek and Thierry really stand out, but I'm not saying they were a lot quicker than the other guys. It's all very marginal. Hobbo was always really quick. Brian Redman. We were all pretty much the same. We weren't out there to try to show each other how good we were; we were all very, very similar. And the same with Tim Schenken. Tim was very, very quick.'

How about Jacky Ickx?

'I never drove with Jacky but I don't think he was as quick as Thierry Boutsen. Don't get me wrong: Jacky was very, very quick, but he always had incredible machinery. You have to remember that.

'He was nowhere near as quick as Stefan Bellof in the same car. You know, Bellof was definitely quicker than Jacky. Jochen Mass was as quick as Jacky, wasn't he? And Derek Bell was as quick as Jacky.

'I wouldn't put Jacky Ickx at the top of my list, but I didn't have personal experience of driving with him.'

Bellof seemed, by most accounts, to be pretty crazy or very brave.

'Well, yes. I don't know about crazy, but I think he was certainly brave. And he was certainly on the edge all the time. In fact, that race at the Nürburgring, the 1,000km in '83, I was out there in my Porsche 956. He was in the Rothmans car and he overtook me down the straight, down the long straight going down to the pits. I was a little way behind him and when I got around to Pflanzgarten, I was there just in time to see his car settling down after he'd taken off and gone end over end.

'The Nürburgring was a place where you didn't really drive at ten-tenths – you just left a little bit in reserve. But I don't think he knew what that meant, really. He was fabulously quick, but he was just an accident looking for somewhere to happen, tragically. But he was a very nice, very quiet, unassuming lad. He was always quicker than Jacky and Jochen.'

How about Martin Brundle?
'I did drive with Martin in the TWR Jaguars. I didn't do all the races with the Jaguars because I had my Porsche commitments as well. He was certainly quicker than I was in Tom's Jaguars, but there wasn't a lot in it. I expected him to be quicker; he was a Formula One driver, he'd driven the cars, developed the cars. He was quick in those cars. He was Tom's star driver.

'Martin and I drove together at Donington in the XJ-S. Before we started the race, we had a little briefing from Tom. I think it was a four-hour race – a round of the European Touring Car Championship.'

It was very wet, wasn't it?
'You're right. I'd forgotten that it was very wet. During the briefing that Tom gave us, he said, "Now, don't forget – when you feel the thing stuttering a bit and it's running out of fuel, don't forget that little switch under the dashboard, which releases the fuel from the secret auxiliary fuel tank." And I thought, "I don't like that very much." That's why we won the race so easily.

'The thing was, all my pals were driving the BMWs. And it was halfway through the season. I spoke to Tom before we went to the next race and said, "Count me out. I'm not doing this anymore." He said to me, "Why not?" I said, "You know very well why not – we're cheating. I don't want to do that."

Fitzpatrick – pictured wagging a wheel at Monza in 1973 – was never as happy with the works Capri as his teammate Jochen Mass. (Motorsport Images)

So I didn't drive for him anymore. And that was it.'

Very honourable.
'They were all my pals. And we were cheating. It just wasn't right. I mean, Tom couldn't lie straight in bed. He couldn't. He was a great driver, though, a super driver.'

I was going to ask you what he was like as a driver.
'He was very good. I was a little bit quicker than he was, but only marginally. He was a fantastic businessman. He could talk the hind legs off a donkey. He was very believable [laughing] but, as I say, he couldn't lie straight in bed!'

Could I take you back to the early days of saloon cars, touring cars, and talk to you about the chaps who were involved in those days? The first one who comes to mind is Andy Rouse.
'Yes, I spent a lot of time with Andy. Andy was very good, a good development driver, good engineer. Super guy – really, really first-class guy. But his whole career was dependent on Ralph Broad, wasn't it? So I think he felt a loyalty to Broadspeed. And that limited his career really, but he was very, very quick and a good development driver as well. I drove with him in the big [Jaguar] XJ Coupés.

'The problem with those was that Leyland delivered them to Broadspeed in, say, January and said, "We're going racing in March", which was ridiculous. So we spent the whole year developing them. By the end of the year, they were really quick and pretty reliable. When Ralph asked me to drive, I was really enthusiastic because I'd had a long career with Ralph Broad. He said,

Fitzpatrick and Tom Walkinshaw shared the winning BMW at the 1976 Silverstone 6 Hours. 'Fitz' later drove a Jaguar XJ-S for the burly Scot. (Motorsport Images)

"Who do you want to drive with you?" I said, "Well, Tim Schenken." I knew Tim. I'd been doing quite a bit with Tim in the Porsches and that sort of thing. Tim's a super guy, very personable, very quick with good feeling for the car, and so he put Tim in. The funny thing was, we decided to take it in turns to start and I don't think the other driver ever got in the car! It never lasted that long. The joke was: "It's Silverstone next week; I'm starting so don't bother to come!"

'I remember we were at Monza: I think it was first race of the [second] year. We were on pole, first and second on the grid, and then in the last qualifying session both the cars blew up. We're still on the grid as first and second but we didn't have the cars so we couldn't race. The following morning, we all went off to the airport early to go home – Ralph and all drivers and everybody.

'There was a glass partition between Arrivals and Departures. We were on the Departures side, waiting to get on the British Airways plane that had just landed. As we're standing there, the plane gets offloaded and all of the British Leyland press people come off the plane, all happy about seeing their cars on pole position. And there's the whole team waiting to get on the plane to go home [laughing]. It was absolutely hysterical. Schenken and I had a really good laugh about that.

'The whole thing was a disaster. If they'd given us another year, we'd have walked everything. They were just too eager to get on the track and get some publicity.'

Back in the 1960s, you were competing against Jim Clark, weren't you?
'Well, I was not really competing against Jim Clark. I was in the same races as Jim Clark. I was in the works Mini Coopers and he was in the works Lotus Cortinas. I must say he was a super guy, very friendly. He was really just one of the guys. I remember halfway through the season, we suddenly went from having, like, 1,100cc engines to 1,300cc engines, which made a massive difference. I remember in practice, I think it was at Silverstone, I was in the now-quicker Mini Cooper. I saw him in the mirror and he caught me up and overtook, and I got into his slipstream. He looked up in the mirror and was really shocked to see that I was there. As soon as we got out of the cars in the collection area, he came over and said, "Fitz, what the hell's happened to your car? I can't believe how fast it suddenly is."

'Jim Clark was a very low-key, super guy. You couldn't meet a nicer guy anywhere. The thing for me, which was so fantastic, was that this was my first year, really, in international racing full-time. So I was a nobody who'd just arrived. But Jim Clark was World Champion, and he was like one of my best mates. He was incredible. He was a really, really nice fellow with no side on him. You'd never ever dream he was a World Champion. A tragedy [that he died racing]. People like that you just want to see them grow old and enjoy life, don't you?

'Now Graham Hill, who drove with him in those Lotus Cortinas – there was nothing wrong with him but he was nowhere near the same sort of guy. Graham didn't mix very much with all the other guys. Not saying that he wasn't a nice guy. He was, he was fine, but he was nothing like Jimmy.'

How about Anita Taylor?
'You couldn't not mention Anita. She was amazingly fast. When Ralph told me she was coming into the team, I thought, "Oh dear, we've got a girl coming into the team" [laughing]. I'd seen her in club racing and that sort of thing. But Ford was very keen to have her along. The first time we got out in the cars, and she got on the track, I realised that I'd have to watch out. I mean, she really was quick. And she was a lovely girl, a really, really nice girl. No question about it: she was really quick.'

Do you think the spirit of camaraderie in those days was much stronger because it was so much more dangerous than today?
'No, I don't think so. I don't think the element of danger brought drivers together, if that's what you mean.'

Fitzpatrick (second right) with 1977 Leyland teammates Tim Schenken and Derek Bell, plus a BMW interloper far left in the shape of Gunnar Nilsson. (Motorsport Images)

What about 'Gentleman' Jack Sears?
'I didn't know Jack very well. I was obviously in a lot of the same races as him but never really competed directly against him. But he was as his nickname – a gentleman. A really, really nice, first-class guy who spoke to everybody. And obviously very quick, especially in the Cobra. Not just the Galaxie but in the Cobra he was terrific.'

Did you have much to do with Sir John Whitmore at that time?
'Well, it was John Whitmore who was responsible for my career, really. I was doing club racing in Minis and there was a race at Silverstone, which combined the British Saloon Car Championship cars, before I was in it, and the club racers. I was in my Mini club racer, which was built by Broadspeed – a really quick car. John Whitmore was in the works Mini Cooper, and I was all over him in the race.

'That's where I met him. He came up to me in the paddock afterwards for a chat and he said, "Wow, you're going well in that car." I said, "Thanks, I'm really enjoying it." He said, "What are you doing next year?" I said, "Well, probably the same sort of thing."

At the 1983 Le Mans 24 Hours, Fitzpatrick finished fifth overall, sharing his Porsche 956 with Guy Edwards and Rupert Keegan. (Motorsport Images)

He said, "I'm going to drive for Ford next year. BMC and Coopers will be looking for a driver to replace me. So if you're interested, I'll put your name forward."

'I got the phone call to go down and see John Cooper, who was the nicest man you would ever wish to meet. Offered me the drive. I think they gave me £100 a race and expenses, which was £100 more than I'd ever had before.

'I drove with Paddy [Hopkirk]. I think that was 1964 – I drove with Paddy in the British Saloon Car Championship. That was my first international series, and it was down to John Whitmore completely.'

How did you find Paddy?
'I got on very well with Paddy. I think he resented the fact that I was a little bit quicker than he was. He wasn't too thrilled about that, because he had just won the Monte Carlo Rally so he was the star, really. He was a bit of a superstar.'

It's interesting, isn't it, that very few people have really done well in rallying and racing?
'Jimmy Clark was probably the main one, wasn't he? I mean, I drove with Roger Clark one year in the Broadspeed. Roger came and did some races in the Escort and he was quick. He wasn't quite as quick as Trevor Taylor, who was also with us in the team. Nobody came out of rallying to be a superstar [on the track] did they? [It was] mainly people from racing who did quite well at rallying, like Jimmy Clark.'

The only exception to that, perhaps, was Vic Elford?
'I think you're probably right. I never drove with Vic in the same car. I drove in the same team as him. Vic really was at the top of the tree in both. I think in Formula One, he never got the right car, but you look at Vic in the 917s and he was very quick.'

You've described a number of the guys you raced against as being extremely nice people. Is there anybody you felt was difficult and not so pleasant, or a bit aggressive, or had ego problems?

'Probably the worst guy that I came across, and drove against, was John Paul in America. His son, John Paul Jr, was very nice, very quick, quicker than his dad. But before he came along, John Paul Snr was racing and I was racing against him.

'He was bad news. Basically, he was a drug dealer. That's what he was, as most of those IMSA drivers were. The three Whittington brothers – I think they all got locked up eventually. John Paul Snr certainly got locked up. Most of the IMSA grid, when I was doing it in the late '70s, was [financed by] drug money. It was incredible. They'd all arrive in their Learjets. There were some real characters over there. They have a name for IMSA – the International Marijuana Smugglers Association!'

What about Bob Wollek?

'Bob was remarkably quick – certainly as quick as anybody. I remember when I was driving with Bob, I used to have to be on really top form to do the same lap times as him. He was very, very quick, but he was a very strange guy. Very, very quiet. Quite an emotional guy. Smoked like hell; always got a cigarette on the go. But very nice guy; never had any problem with him.

'I drove with him a lot as a co-driver and in separate cars. He was as quick as anybody in the [Porsche] 935s, which was where I was driving with him. But a very introverted character.'

You mentioned Jochen Mass, who has a great sense of humour these days.

'He is a super guy. Always had a lot of fun with Jochen and [he was] very quick. I drove for Ford Germany with him in the BDA Escort. I think we won a couple of races together in that. And then in the Capris. To be honest, that Capri was the worst car I ever drove. It was a horrendous car. He'd done a lot of the testing with it and he seemed to handle it well, but I was never happy in the Capri. I mean, it was always up on one leg or two wheels. They sorted it eventually but by the time they sorted it I'd moved on to BMW.

'Jochen was very nice, very friendly, super guy, and very quick. Never quite got into the right car in Formula One, did he? I'm not sure he was quite good enough for Formula One, I wouldn't know. But he just never seemed to get into the right car.

'Certainly in the 956s and 962s, he was very fast. He wasn't as quick as Stefan Bellof. Bellof was definitely quicker than most of them. In fact, if I remember, at the Nürburgring 1,000km he was six or seven seconds quicker than Jochen or Jacky. That's a lot, even at the Nürburgring. But he ended up rolling the thing into a ball, so he was obviously over the limit.'

Did you drive against Jackie Oliver very much?

'No. Jackie was a bit of a difficult character. I was never friendly with him. I was never not friends with him – I was never fussed. I thought he was a bit hard. At our level, he was quick, but he never quite made it in Formula One. He was quite an aggressive sort of chap.'

Was anybody exceptionally quick in the wet? Did anybody stand out as being particularly good when it rained?

'Well, I always thought I was good in the wet! People used to say I was good in the wet. I think Bellof was, but he was quick everywhere, just looking for somewhere to have an accident. He was on the edge all the time. You can't really drive like that. It didn't bother me if it was wet. In fact I was more than happy if it was wet, because a lot of guys didn't like it.

'I think Brian Redman was a pretty underrated driver. He was very quick in those 917s, but he never really got the right car in Formula One. You couldn't meet a nicer guy than Brian. He had his share of accidents and knocked himself about but he's all right now.

'There was nothing to choose between us, really. It depended on what you had for breakfast in the morning, or what time you got up. Of all those guys you've mentioned, I was always more than happy to drive with any of them, and they all kept you on your toes. I think Martin Brundle was exceptional. Wollek was very good, but he was just a strange character.'

Somebody we haven't touched on is 'de Cad' – Alain de Cadenet.

'I never drove with him. I liked him, though. He was a very nice guy. And he was certainly quick. I don't know *how* quick he was, but he was certainly a character and he was part of the scene.'

Of course, he drove with Chris Craft.

'Chris was always really quick. He was a big pal of Keith Greene's. They were both Essex lads and his face didn't fit in, somehow. I drove with him for a couple of years at Broadspeed, and he was really good. And he was a very, very nice fella, but he was a bit of a Jack-the-Lad.

'He was very put out when Jaguars came in, or Leyland [as the cars were called!] came in, and wanted Broadspeed to run the cars. Ralph Broad wanted me to drive with Chris, and they wouldn't have Chris. Nothing to do with his driving because he was bloody good. That's why Ralph said to me, "Who do you want to drive with?"

'That was a shame for Chris. I liked Chris. He was a nice fella.'

You mentioned the crooks in IMSA. Were there any rogues in British motorsport?

'Not on the same level, really. I can remember standing in the pits in Atlanta with a couple of the Whittingtons. It was a practice session. There was an airstrip alongside Atlanta and this Learjet comes down along the main straight in front of the pits – just off the ground, really. I think it was Bill [Whittington] and he said, "God, I've told Louise not to fly as low as that [laughing]!" Incredible. We did have a great time over in IMSA, we really did.

'The thing is in the States, not only is there a lot more money, but there's a lot of people there with a lot of money who are prepared to spend it on motor racing. That was the thing about IMSA: you'd be sitting on the grid with mainly multi-millionaires in the cars. They'd all got so much money and, of course, plenty were drug dealers as well. It was a different scene altogether.'

Hamilton – the modern-day 'rainmaster' – won the 2020 Turkish Grand Prix from sixth place on the grid. (Motorsport Images)

LEWIS HAMILTON

Interviewed by **DAVID TREMAYNE**, courtesy of Mercedes AMG Petronas F1 team

LEWIS HAMILTON (GB)
Born 7 January 1985

Sir Lewis Hamilton is the most successful driver in Grand Prix history, with seven World Championships and 100 race victories at the time of writing. He signed a contract with McLaren while still in karting, and moved up to Formula One with that team after winning the 2006 GP2 Championship. Hamilton very nearly won the F1 title in his rookie season, did win it in 2008, and has been the dominant force in the hybrid era after joining Mercedes in 2013. In 2020, he broke Michael Schumacher's record for most Grand Prix wins, and equalled the great German's tally of seven world titles.

Of all the drivers you've raced against during your career, who has particularly stood out for you?
'I've raced against some brilliant drivers in my time, so it's difficult to pick just one. However, Fernando [Alonso] and Seb [Vettel] definitely stood out in terms of performance.'

Who were the best teammates?
'I've been fortunate to work alongside some of the best. For natural speed, I'd say Fernando, and in terms of an all-round human being, Valtteri [Bottas].'

Which driver do you think was the best of all time and why?
'The best driver of all time, to me, has to be Ayrton Senna. He inspired me so much as a kid, I was in awe of him. Watching him race always inspired me to work even harder.'

Who did you have the most fun with?
'I've had a lot of fun with my teammates over the years. Some of the most fun days were when Nico [Rosberg] and I were in karting when we were younger.'

Who was the bravest?
'That's a tough question. To race at the speeds we do, I'd say all racing drivers are pretty brave...'

Do you have any favourite stories about fellow drivers?
'Spending so much time with the other drivers over the years, we've created some great memories. However, it's been challenging over the past year [2020], because COVID restrictions have kept us from spending time together. But we have a lot of exciting races ahead of us this season [2021] and I hope restrictions continue to ease, so we can continue making more.'

What has been the biggest disappointment in your career?
'That would probably be losing my first championship, in 2007.'

> 'The best driver of all time, to me, has to be Ayrton Senna. He inspired me so much as a kid, I was in awe of him. Watching him race always inspired me to work even harder.'

MARTIN BRUNDLE

Interviewed by **PHILIP PORTER**

> **MARTIN BRUNDLE (GB)**
> Born 1 June 1959
>
> Brundle served a varied motorsport apprenticeship that included a stint as teammate to Stirling Moss in the British Saloon Car Championship, but really announced his arrival as a future star during a famous duel with Ayrton Senna for the 1983 British Formula Three Championship. He graduated to Formula One with Tyrrell the following year – alongside fellow young hot-shoe Stefan Bellof – but badly injured his ankles in a crash at Detroit. Brundle's F1 teammates included Michael Schumacher (1993) and Mika Häkkinen (1994), and he won the 1988 World Sports Car Championship with the TWR-Jaguar team, with which he also won the 1990 Le Mans 24 Hours.

Who was your favourite teammate?

'Ah, that would be Mark Blundell, undoubtedly. We were very close and had a lot of fun together. We were like blood brothers. In sports car racing, you have to work with each other, to trust each other and leave the ego behind a little bit.

'And you know, if you're in a Le Mans 24-hour race, you need to know that the other driver won't be bouncing across the kerbs if you've agreed not to use them, or ground it, or be bouncing off backmarkers, and you've got to set the car up to fit three different sizes of driver and [suit different] driving styles and what have you. So, it's a complex business, motorsport teammates.'

Who do you think was the bravest?

'Well, what does bravery mean in a racing car? You can be a risk-taker. Does that equate to bravery, as such, or is that a bit foolhardy? I will go with Stefan Bellof on that. He did appear to be absolutely fearless and had a trust and a belief in his own abilities. Obviously, he flipped the Porsche at the Nürburgring. And he'd had a few big shunts. He did live life on the edge. You've got to question whether that's bravery or foolhardiness. Back in the day, in terms of teammates, I think it would have to be Bellof who had that devil-may-care attitude.

'I think true bravery would have been in the 1950s and '60s when there were no seatbelts, no crash barriers, often just trees, and the mortality rate was massive. I think that's the true meaning of bravery in a racing car, because you know your chances of dying, just through mechanical failure, or coming across something on the track, are incredibly high. When you hear those stories about how the drivers hoped to get thrown out of the cars as their best chance of surviving, thinking that when you step into a car, knowing that may well happen to you, then that's, for me, the true meaning of driving bravery.'

Do you have any favourite stories about fellow drivers?

'Well, yes, you have a few laughs along the way, there's no doubt about it. With some of them, I guess it's what goes on the road, stays on the road.

'Mark Blundell and I were at Imola when we were teammates. I finished third that day for Ligier but he crashed on the first lap. So I'd had a great day and I got a great big trophy, which is sitting in my cabinet today. It was 1993 and I was larking around pulling the handbrake on as we were leaving the *péage*, the toll at the *autopista*, and a policeman tried to put his little red bat out to stop us and we didn't know what that meant at the time.

'Eventually we got pulled over on the motorway and they pulled Mark out of the car. I'm sitting in the car with my wife and my trainer, and Mark's beginning to get money out of his pocket to pay a fine. When he gave his name, they said, in broken English, "You just finished third in the Grand Prix at Imola," and Mark suddenly twigged. He realised they'd got the names mixed up and came running back to the car and said, "Gimme the trophy, gimme the trophy." And he goes marching over with this massive trophy from Imola, and shows it to them: "Yeah, yeah, me in third place." Then I saw the cash coming back out of the window and a handshake and off we went!

'I remember picking up Michael Schumacher in my Jet Ranger helicopter one day. We were flying to Silverstone and we went over Blenheim Palace. And Michael said, "England's beautiful. I had no idea. I thought England was ugly." OK! I think he thought Blenheim Palace was probably somebody's rather nice house and garden.

'I was thinking about it later on. Why did he suddenly say that? We were flying over the beautiful green countryside of the UK, which I knew so well. And then I realised that his experience of England at that point had been Heathrow, the M1 and Silverstone paddock, basically. And I realised he had a very concrete view of the UK.

'Michael was good fun. We used to joke about him being first out of the taxi and last into the bar, and all that sort of thing. But he was a good guy. And yeah, we had some fun together.

Brundle and Jan Lammers finished second in the 1988 Spa 1,000km in the Jaguar XJR-9. Brundle took that year's drivers' title. (Motorsport Images)

'There was the one with Mark Blundell in the private jet when we were both reading the paper on the way home, pretending the other one wasn't there after we'd had an incident together on track at Estoril. But Blundell had the last laugh because I went to get on a plane in Nagoya one night to go to Australia. I had a First Class ticket. I handed

> **'I often say Senna knew where the grip was before and during a corner, and mere mortals like ourselves knew where the grip was during and after a corner.'**

my ticket in and the lady said to me, in sort of Japanese English, "You're already on the plane." And I said, "Well, I'm not because I'm here. I'm standing here." "No, you're already on the plane." We walked on and Mark Blundell was sat in my seat in First Class. He'd told everybody the story, so they all raised a glass of Champagne to me. I spent the night in 32J at the back of the plane, in Mark's seat because he wouldn't shift. So he very much had the last laugh in my First Class seat from Nagoya to Adelaide.'

What are your memories of Ayrton Senna? He was ultra-competitive, of course, but broke the rules a bit. In your F3 season together, he tried to take you off once or twice. It was so extraordinary: he had the ability and yet he felt he had to also behave like that.
'Ayrton had the greatest God-given talent I've ever seen. It was just natural with him, it was just easy for him. He talked about Monaco, being out of the car watching himself driving, he got into such a rhythm, which I understand. I know that feeling, but I've never experienced it to the extreme where you imagine you're watching yourself, but you do get into a bit of a trance around a place like Monaco in a Formula One car, as you're just bouncing from bump to kerb to manhole cover and grazing the barriers and you get into an incredible rhythm. So I understand what he means but he had another level.

'I remember an experience in Formula Three: it's a very long story, but it sums him up. We had a race at Silverstone in the rain. I took off from second on the grid; he was on pole, which often happened, and then I overtook him. I went down to Stowe, and it was treacherous conditions. He went sailing down the outside into Stowe Corner when it was a really fast right-hander. I saw him and I thought, "At sea, you wouldn't want to be out there." I navigated the corner very nicely on the racing line. He went right around the outside and came out in the lead, in front of me.

'That was the karting line. I never did karting; I did banger racing when I was young. In karting – I used to have to save up for the magazine, let alone the kart – it's established that you often actually go off the racing line where the rubber makes the track slick and all that, but this was an extreme example of that, all the way around the outside of Stowe in the pouring rain.

'The race was red-flagged because a guy called Enrique Mansilla had a big crash. So when we regrouped to head out for the second part of the race, I thought, "I'm going to try Senna's line." I went down the outside into Stowe. This was the lap to the grid for the restart. Hit the biggest puddle of water, aquaplaned, went down the grass, just kept it out of the bank, grazed the barriers, survived it, got back to the grid. This time Senna beat me away. He finished first and I finished second, and on the podium I said to him, "Your line into Stowe didn't work in the second part of the race, did it?" Then he said, "I don't know. I didn't try it. It was too wet. There was too much standing water."

'The whole track looked like it was flooded. So he kind of had that sixth sense. I often say Senna knew where the grip was before and during a corner, and mere mortals like ourselves knew where the grip was during and after a corner.

'That's why he was so awesome in the qualifying days with the turbocharged cars and qualifying tyres, which was an adventure from the first corner to the last corner. You've suddenly got 400 or 500 horsepower more with the turbos [turned up] and a set of tyres that's good for five miles –

Senna in the process of taking both himself and Brundle out of the race at Oulton Park in 1983. Their Formula Three battle that year (far left) was a classic. (Motorsport Images)

and you've got to get the best out of them. So it's feeling your way round, really, with 1,300 horsepower...

'He had this gift and I think it showed up through so many of his greatest wins – his first victory in Estoril in the Lotus [in 1985], for example. So he had this God-given talent. He was a paradox. He was one of the first guys that would think of driving you off the road. And then the first guy to jump out of the car and run back and check that you were OK. He had a competitive spirit that was fearsome, but he also had a human side to him.

'The day he died, we were all shocked. I remember the day Jim Clark died because I was with my dad on a rally. But the day Senna died as a Formula One driver, we all thought, "Well, if it can happen to him, it can happen to anybody," just as I'm sure all the guys did back in the '60s when Jim Clark lost his life.

How did Schumacher compare to Senna?
'I would say Senna was driven from the heart and Schumacher driven from the head. Michael came at it in a different way. He wasn't emotionally driven at all. He worked incredibly hard. I don't think he'd got quite the natural gift of driving or the speed of Ayrton, not quite, but he worked much harder in galvanising everybody in the team around him, everything was pointed at him. And he delivered on track, so they loved him. You forget that everybody in, for example, Formula One is competitive, whether it's the truckie, the mechanics, the new guys in the team, the old hands – everybody in a team is super-competitive. And of course, if you're winning, then it points at you. Michael was just extremely good in the car and out of the car to make

sure everything was pointing in his direction and then just delivered.

'He had the speed and critically he had the fitness. He turned up in Formula One off the back of an era when we were used to protecting tyres, brakes, clutches, gearboxes, engines… just generally you had to sort of babysit a Formula One car to get it to the end: there were very, very high rates of unreliability. Michael turned up as the cars were getting more robust and much stronger, and could drive every corner of every lap absolutely flat-out. He just moved the game on, frankly. So he was the right man for the right era, and was smart enough to make the most of it.'

And finally, how about a few thoughts on Nigel Mansell?

'Nigel, what a character! Most sports people I've met over the decades – I would say the vast percentage, and I definitely fell into this category – you're driven because you're constantly dissatisfied with what you've achieved or how you drove the car, how you read this race or whatever. I'm sure [it's true] whichever sport you're in and it just drives you to be better and better and better by being completely dissatisfied with what you've achieved at all times. You end up delivering something that other people can't imagine how you do it: you drive a Formula One car around Monaco in qualifying, you do 240mph down the Mulsanne Straight, before the chicanes [were added], in the pouring rain in the middle of the night. It's one of those things you do that felt absolutely normal but are obviously extraordinary feats for sports people. That's basically how you drive yourself.

'There are a few percent, a smaller percentage of people, who have a supreme self-confidence and that was Nigel, for me, in terms of his belief. A very strong man. And again, the right man for the right time because the early '90s cars were so unbelievably physical. They had no power steering on them; they were unbelievably physical cars to drive.

'I remember stepping in for Nigel at Spa in 1988, when he had chickenpox, in the Williams Judd and they gave me a steering wheel that looked like a doughnut. I literally

Brundle at the 1992 Australian Grand Prix – he finished third in his final race for Benetton – and (below) with Nigel Mansell in 1985. (Motorsport Images)

stepped in at the last minute. I sat in Nigel's seat, got in and they put the steering wheel on. I'm like, "What is this?" I could barely turn the wheel to get it out of the garage. It was Nigel's steering wheel, a tiny little thing because he was so physically strong, and you had to be because there was no balancing up of driver weights back then, so Nigel was carrying many, many kilos more than an Alain Prost, for example.

'They were such brutal cars to drive and Nigel's confidence and sheer strength and determination made him the right man for the time. His junior racing career was fairly lacklustre in many respects but he ended up being a World Champion through sheer guts, determination and self-belief, and speed. He had the speed and the bravery to go with it. I'm not sure there was a huge amount of finesse but there was certainly some great delivery from Nigel. Yeah, he was a remarkable individual.'

STIRLING MOSS

Interviewed by **PHILIP PORTER** between 2005 and 2010

SIR STIRLING MOSS (GB)
Born 17 September 1929
Died 12 April 2020

Universally recognised as one of the greatest drivers of all time, Moss was also perhaps the most versatile, competing at the top level in rallying, sports cars and Formula One. His first Championship-level victory came at the 1955 British GP when he was Juan Manuel Fangio's teammate at Mercedes-Benz. Moss also won that year's Mille Miglia, Targa Florio and Tourist Trophy – the last-named being one of seven TT victories that he would amass. He lost the 1958 World Championship to Mike Hawthorn by a single point, but after Fangio's retirement that year, Moss was the sport's acknowledged benchmark. Sadly, however, his career was cut short by an accident at Goodwood in April 1962.

When you joined Vanwall in 1957, your teammate was Tony Brooks.
'I think that Tony is the best driver in the world that has never been really well-known to the general public. If I had to make up a team of drivers, a team that would run single-seaters and sports cars, I think I would take Tony above anybody else, anybody else in the world, including Fangio. If it was Formula One only, I would take Fangio. But Tony was right up there: an enormous adaptability, very careful with the car without being slow.

'I think he was very good, excellent. I can never remember seeing Tony in a fluster at all, about anything.'

Very British!
'Yes, but even more so than that. Tony was just... phlegmatic? Very easy-going without being subservient in any way. He would drive a car up to its limit and not really complain if it was bad, if it had a flat spot or whatever. It didn't really seem to worry him.'

And you had a good relationship?
'Yes. I don't think he was very pleased with the fact that I had the number-one contract. My contract gave me permission to take over his car and so on, or change this and that. I don't think that made him very happy.'

But you were the established man and he was still really on his way up.
'Yes, I was. That is why I think he accepted it. Let me put it this way – I think that he would have preferred that it wasn't like that!'

Part of the character of a racing driver is to be intensely competitive, isn't it? He doesn't come over as quite being so competitive, but presumably he was?
'Yes. I must say he didn't come over as being a very competitive driver until he began racing. He wasn't outspoken or anything at all. He was just a very nice, ordinary person.'

Stuart Lewis-Evans was the third member of that Vanwall team in 1957 and '58.
'Very good. I don't think he was very fit, or perhaps strong is a better word. I think that one of the problems was that the races were then two hours minimum and quite a lot were hot. I think that was a problem for him because I don't think he was a well person, but there was no doubt he was an enormous talent. In fact, I think he was probably the bravest of all three of us. I think that if anybody was going to take a corner that was nearly flat and try it out flat first, I think Stuart would. He had quite a lot of guts, actually.'

It was a very strong team, wasn't it?
'Yes, very strong. Strong as any team that I can think of.'

Your title rival in 1958 was Mike Hawthorn. Was there a bit of friendly rivalry between you?
'Oh yes. Well, Mike was English – you were either a Hawthorn or a Moss fan, weren't you? Hawthorn was a tall, good-looking, beer-drinking guy. Quite a character, and I was only for the sport. I would give up anything and concentrate only on that. I didn't drink and, you know, appeared far less exciting. There was no doubt he was a very competent driver.'

His performances varied a bit, didn't they?
'That was the problem. On his day he was terrific, but not terribly consistent. He was very fast in sports cars and could be very fast in Formula One, but not always.

'I actually lent him my car to race once! He was quite a good driver, nice bloke, careful with the car, so he was a good person to lend it to. I think people always felt, because there was a rivalry, that we didn't get along, which was not true.

'He certainly had quite a lot of skill. Peter Collins was more reliable – not quite as quick as Mike, but overall probably a better driver to have on a team. He was a consistent Mike, really – very good. I got Pete to drive with me in the Targa [in 1955], a good choice, because he was good. I mean, he did go off the road [but] so did I, so he was going fast enough. The point is, he was fast enough to make mistakes,

Moss and Brooks won the 1958 TT in an Aston Martin DBR/1. Moss rated his quiet, modest teammate incredibly highly. (Motorsport Images)

A young Moss and Hawthorn in 1953. By 1958 (left), they were battling at Monza as title rivals. (Motorsport Images)

but he was also fast enough to be forgiven for making them. Some you can't forgive because they weren't going that quickly, but Pete would be going that quickly, and therefore that is why I chose him.'

You both did a brilliant job to win the 1955 Targa Florio and clinch the World Sports Car Championship for Mercedes-Benz.
'First of all, we were a similar size, so we were OK with the same seat and screen. He was a bit taller than me but it worked out quite well. He was fast and looked after the car. He wasn't the sort of guy to over-rev to show he was quicker than you. I would say one of the better ones. I knew him, of course, in 500s so right the way through. Peter was a very, very competent driver. In the Targa Florio that year, he did a tremendous job.'

If he hadn't been killed, and with Fangio retired, do you think he would have been your main rival?
'More so than Mike Hawthorn, yes. Because (a) I don't think Hawthorn was that fit, and (b) Mike had on days and off days, and when you are racing every week you cannot afford to be like that.'

And what about Innes Ireland?
'A driver who I think was a lot better than most people give him credit for. Innes was really quite fast but he was like Mike in that he would have on days and off days. I don't think he took his racing as seriously on the off days as many other people would.'

He enjoyed life a bit too much?
'Yes, I think so! He really was an enormous character. He certainly was one of the characters of motor racing but I think Innes was very talented. He had a lot of car control. He was like a forerunner of Jean Alesi. Alesi had enormous talent, but he couldn't get it strung together to take a big win. Innes was much the same, I think. He had a lot of talent and he was as quick as Jimmy [Clark] in a similar car.
'I think his biggest problem was Colin [Chapman] was not as keen on him as he was on Jimmy. I think he could see that Innes was a bit of a loose cannon by comparison and he did what most people would do – he settled for the guy that was more reliable.'

Was he tremendous fun? Pretty wild?
'Yes, he was. Half of him was good fun to be with; the other half you would try to ignore. You know, he was one of those people who was a bit of a Jekyll and Hyde.'

During 1961, you and Innes helped each other. He lent you the works [Lotus] for Monza. On another occasion he followed you around because he was struggling to even qualify. You were clearly good pals and very supportive of each other.
'Yes, and he beat me twice with the latest Lotus, at Goodwood in 1960, which just showed that he was right up there when he had a distinct advantage. The Lotus, when it came out, was quite ahead of other cars and he didn't need much advantage to be able to win.'

He had quite a lot of accidents.
'Yes, but don't forget he was driving for Lotus! That is the point.'

Let's talk about Juan Manuel Fangio.
'I have always looked upon Fangio as the greatest F1 driver that ever lived. Naturally I did not see all the drivers, particularly those before the war, but any man who, in his time, could stand so much above his fellow drivers must be great.
'Mike Hawthorn always reckoned that Ascari was the greatest, but I watched both of them and I never thought Ascari was nearly so neat and clean as Fangio. Fangio would take a corner in the same place every time, just missing the straw bales, whereas Ascari would sometimes nudge the bales on straightening out his car. One could say that Fangio was lucky to have had Mercedes in 1954 and 1955, but that is only two years out of the five in which he won the World Championship.
'When he first came over to Europe, he was quite hard on his cars, but in the end he was easier on them because he had so much ability that he did not need to overstress his car. To my mind, he was in his prime in 1955 and 1956, and I had the feeling, in 1957, that he was not enjoying it as much as before, when it had just come naturally and easily.
'I had great respect for Fangio but I never, unfortunately, got to know him as closely as I would have liked to because we could not talk outside racing. This was simply because he did not speak English. I knew a certain amount of Italian, so we could talk about the car, we could talk about food, we could talk about women – not that I can think there is much else one would want to talk about!'

I have a theory about Fangio that he had to be driving an open-wheel car to see the wheels, because not only were you quicker than him in sports cars, but when he was driving the Mercedes-Benz W196 streamliners in the British GP at Silverstone in '54, he kept hitting the marker barrels, which again suggests he needed the wheels to be exposed.
'What you are saying is quite correct, but why? How it could be like that is something I never really got to the bottom of. You don't drive looking at your wheels. They are there and you naturally see them. I was lucky because it doesn't make any difference to me whether the wheels are enclosed

or open; so I can't see how it made any difference. But what you say is absolutely true – he liked open-wheel cars and was at his best with them.'

Was he especially precise, more so than everybody else?
'Yes, oh absolutely. I think he had enormous skill and precision. What made him so good was the fact that whatever he could do, he could continually do. He wouldn't be really good and then taper off. And of course his precision was incredible.'

You mentioned Alberto Ascari as well.
'Ascari I thought was (a) a very nice person, and (b) a very polished driver. I mean, the difference between him and Fangio was really very, very small. I would put Fangio a bit higher because I knew him better. But I think Ascari was of that sort of stature, without doubt.

'I think, generally, in motor racing, including today, there are usually four or five drivers who can win. Then, occasionally, one outsider comes along and upsets the form – like Maurice Trintignant, who won twice, which was amazing. In the early '50s, the four or five would have included Farina, Fangio, González and Ascari. They were up there.

'I don't think Ascari quite had the skill of Fangio but he was an exceptionally good driver. Very tidy, very complete, had quite good stamina, good car control, wouldn't throw it around unnecessarily. He has to be one of the best drivers of all time. I would put him in the top 10.'

Later in your career, you briefly raced against John Surtees. Was he pretty wild to start with?
'Surtees was very wild at the start. He had a tremendous amount of talent and was very fast. I think hard on the machine early on. I think that he learnt a tremendous amount very quickly, because as he slowed up he went just as fast, and then he became World Champion. It showed that he had enormous car control.'

Is there any relationship between racing with two and four wheels, do you think?

Following Fangio at Aintree in 1955. Moss got the better of the Maestro that day to take his first Grand Prix victory. (Motorsport Images)

'I think with strategy and that type of thing, yes, I think there probably is.'

And balance is very important, isn't it?
'I would say so. I don't know that much about him, but I remember saying to Surtees, "Which is safer – a car or a bike?" and he said, "A bike, by miles." I asked why and he said, "If [on a bike] I see an accident about to happen I get off it, I just leave it behind!" I said, "Well, Masten Gregory is a bit like that!" John was a very tough competitor.'

You also had Jim Clark coming through at that time.
'Jimmy Clark was a naturally fast driver and I think the great thing about Jimmy, really, was that he had the right person to work with. In other words, Chapman had sufficient knowledge that he could interpret Jimmy's comments and benefit both of them from it. Jimmy was good enough that whatever car he had, he could get the best that you could out of it.

  'Above all, I think that it was his feedback to Colin that Colin could interpret correctly. They were a great team – probably two of the best driver-designers, period. Jimmy without Colin would have been, not wasted, but he wouldn't have done as well as he did, and I think that Colin without him wouldn't have either. So they were a great pair.'

Presumably, on pure and natural ability, he was the closest to you?
'I think so, yes.'

So head and shoulders, really, above the rest?
'Yes.'

But you didn't fear him as such? You respected him?
'I respected him… At the time I retired, I felt I could just about cope, as I did in Monaco [in 1961], but I could see that he was looming up closer.'

He often had better machinery than you.
'Yes, he did.'

But I guess that he was still learning at this stage?

Moss's Maserati 250F pictured at the Gasworks Hairpin during his winning drive at Monaco in 1956 (far left), and sharing a joke with two great characters – Innes Ireland and Graham Hill. (Motorsport Images)

'Yes. He hadn't been competing for that long when I got out. I am sure that he hadn't reached his zenith when I retired.'

Can I ask you about Graham Hill?
'Graham was a lot of fun. He had a good sense of humour, but he was serious about his driving. He was a man I asked to drive with me on quite a few occasions because he was somebody who would drive to a plan – he wasn't trying to prove how good he was. He'd obviously arrived and that was OK. He was fairly quick; certainly not the fastest driver. He was fast enough for me to want to be with him but he was also someone I could trust. He was not slow, which meant I didn't then have to be hard on the car to make up for him.

'He was a good, fast, natural driver who would really want to win. He was a gutsy sort of bloke. He seemed to me to be a bloke who was conscientious and intelligent – thought about things – and would contribute to the drive by having ideas. From my point of view, he was a good person to share a drive with.

'At Le Mans [in 1961], I think we were doing exceptionally well. I don't know where we would have finished but we were doing far more than one would have thought a GT car could do, because I think we were both consistent and fast all the time.

'There was a serious side when you were discussing things that mattered. When they didn't matter, he was always larking around. He was just a likeable bloke to be around with a great sense of humour.

'I was not surprised when he won the World Championship. He was a man of considerable ability. He wasn't a racer, which was just as well, because I wouldn't have wanted a racer to be with me – they are going to try to show they can be quicker than me. I think Graham was content to drive with me and do as well as he could. He wasn't full of ego. It wasn't an ego trip. Very mature and intelligent.'

Was finding the right co-driver at Le Mans an important consideration?
'One of the problems with Le Mans is finding another driver with whom you are happy to share the car. You do a stint of driving and you go carefully, as required. Then you give it to the other driver and he goes out. When he comes back in at the end of his stint, he says, "I am sorry but the whatever isn't working now." It is not necessarily his fault but you feel, "Christ, it was better than that when I gave it to you."'

How did driving styles vary?
'There were quite a few drivers who would make a manoeuvre that I wouldn't, I would wait. Roy Salvadori would dart in somewhere where I thought it would have been more politic to wait but he didn't mind too much.

'There weren't that many dirty drivers but there were a few, but I let them know that they had better not do that to me. I'd do that by going up and telling them, "I think what you did was not right and you'd better not do it to me, otherwise you are going to go off." It was as simple as that. "I am not going to be the one who gets pushed around. I don't intend to be dirty, but I am not going to accept it from you." I think that's acceptable.'

IMAGE CREDITS

ALL IMAGES CREDITED where captioned, apart from:

Page 4 collage
Row 1:   Image 1 to 6 Michael Cole
Row 2:   Image 1 to 4 Michael Cole; image 5 and 6 Motorsport Images
Row 3:   Image 1 to 6 Motorsport Images
Row 4:   Image 1 to 3 Ian Wagstaff; image 4 Steve Slater; image 5 Mobil PR; image 6 Corporate Archives Porsche AG
Row 5:   Image 1 and 2 Steve Havelock; image 3 to 5 Newspress; image 6 John Fitzpatrick collection

Page 6	Motorsport Images
Page 14	Steve Slater
Page 36	Mobil PR
Page 53	Steve Havelock
Page 87	Ian Wagstaff
Page 111	Motorsport Images

Back cover (Clockwise from top left)
Motorsport Images; Brian Kent Joscelyne Collection; Motorsport Images; Corporate Archives Porsche AG; Motorsport Images